Ron Bowman

# THE LONELY HEART

*By the same author*

SECRETS OF ANSWERED PRAYER

# THE LONELY HEART

*The Answer to the Problem
of Loneliness through Life*

by

**CYRIL  H.  POWELL**

**M.Litt., Ph.D.**

**ABINGDON PRESS**

NEW YORK  •  NASHVILLE

*First Edition 1960*

© — Arthur James Ltd. — 1960

MADE AND PRINTED IN GREAT BRITAIN BY PURNELL AND SONS, LTD.,
PAULTON (SOMERSET) AND LONDON

He came to the desert of London town
  Grey miles long;
He wandered up and he wandered down,
  Singing a quiet song.

He came to the desert of London town,
  Mirk miles broad;
He wandered up and he wandered down
  Ever alone with God.

There were thousands and thousands of human kind
  In this desert of brick and stone:
But some were deaf and some were blind,
  And he was there alone.

At length the good hour came; he died
  As he had lived, alone:
He was not missed from the desert wide—
  Perhaps he was found at the Throne.

*William Blake* by JAMES THOMSON

# DEDICATION

To the one who more than any other
has put an infinite distance between
me and the experience of loneliness.

# Foreword

LONELINESS is a sad and widespread malady. The word conjures up for many the thought of elderly men and women, isolated in tiny flats in crowded cities, and, through circumstance or bereavement, lacking the companionship of a mate, and feeling unwanted and unloved. For them loneliness is poignant and serious enough to be classified as a psychological illness. And the amount an outsider can do is small. The visit of a minister or friend once or twice a week, welcomed and valuable as it is, is no real solution of the difficulty. Think of all the other hours of day and night! I think I should dread the morning when I contemplated the blank hours of a day that stretched before me, and thought, "What on earth shall I do today?" The newspaper, the book, the little walk, the visit to a shop drawn out as long as possible—how unsatisfying they are! How futile!

Yet loneliness is not circumscribed by this class of sufferer. The young can be intolerably lonely. The boys and girls at boarding school, who join it after others of their age have already established friendships; the undergraduate or college student, in the front rank amongst the boys or girls at school, and then plunged into a milieu where the standard is frighteningly higher and where the bright school prize-winner feels a duffer and loses his self-esteem and confidence—what loneliness is here! Even suicide is not uncommon as the dons of any residential university will tell you.

There is the boy or girl newly at work in warehouse or factory, shipyard or office, shyly and secretly setting out with high ideals, perhaps, and then, out of sheer loneliness,

7

making the wrong friends or succumbing to the lower moral level and feeling terribly lonely and torn by conflict —the conflict between wanting to be a strong character standing up for the vision of his heart and wanting fiercely to be loved and liked by the rest.

So one could go on. Most of us are lonely at some time or another and little has been written to help us. I know Dr. Powell. He writes with insight and sympathy and longs to help. He enriches his book with his knowledge of the lives of others, famous and humble. He quotes frequently from his own experience. Above all, he helps us most as he guides us to "the God who brings the lonely home". This is the best treatment of loneliness that I have read.

*Minister of the City Temple,*   LESLIE D. WEATHERHEAD.
*London.*

# Contents

# CONTENTS

## PART III

## LONELINESS AND GOD

# I

# A Universal Problem

*... It isn't that I want to be alone,*
*But that everyone's alone—or so it seems to me.*

T. S. ELIOT

SOME years ago news was released of a human tragedy that immediately caught public attention.

The landlady of a dingy lodging-house in Battersea came home one night earlier than was expected. On opening the door, she sniffed the unmistakable smell of gas. Rushing to the kitchen, she found all the oven taps turned off. But the smell was not coming from there: it was seeping down the narrow stairs.

With the help of a burly neighbour a locked door on the landing above was burst open. The action was in the nick of time. With the speedy arrival of a doctor, ambulance men, and the skilled attention of the local hospital, the lodger from the gas-filled room revived. "Another couple of minutes and he'd have been dead," the thronging reporters were told.

In this case the press was more than ordinarily interested, for the name of the lodger had been a household word. The public soon forgets, and this man, who had been a well-known actor, had suffered first from neglect and then oblivion. It seemed incredible that so famous a figure could have faded into obscurity and penury in so short a time. As a result of the ensuing publicity, not only was this man cared for on leaving hospital and placed in surroundings more befitting his former reputation, but considerable fresh support was given to a number of funds and good causes that exist to prevent such tragedies.

In that shabby back room a note was found on the dressing-table. It would have been the first exhibit at a coroner's inquest had the suicide gone as planned. One sentence read: "I am taking the only way out of this hell of loneliness."

There can be little doubt that in this instance the problems many have to face, of living without satisfying work, adequate status and a background of relations and friends, were aggravated by the dramatic change in this man's circumstances. Someone who had known the adulation of crowds and never been without company, found himself drifting fast into no-man's-land. What he experienced and admitted was a "hell of loneliness".

I have high-lighted this story of a forgotten actor to show the poignancy of loneliness as it comes home to an individual. But the problem is universal. It can be approached on a world scale. The lonely are to be found among the street-dwellers of Calcutta, on Skid Row in the Bowery district of New York, in refugee camps throughout the world, in Battersea and Soho. Nor should those lounging in Shepherds Hotel, Cairo, the Waldorf-Astoria, New York, and the Ritz, London, be forgotten, for the rich and the idle sometimes live in strange isolation; nor those in farms and villages in every part of the world; nor those in outposts and remote places. And somewhere in this picture, midway between all these extremes, are thousands of folk like ourselves. To us all at times loneliness becomes a problem.

In spite of this the peoples of the world are not yet sufficiently awake to its urgency. Loneliness is not something we can see. Its ravages do not plainly and directly affect the body. It is pre-eminently a state of mind. One would have thought, however, that the mischief it does is evident enough. Apart from the acute distress it causes, it leads to maladjustments of all kinds, and sometimes to chronic mental ill-health. Over the years, as our opening story reminds us, it has been responsible for numberless suicides. A mountainous list of excesses, mistakes, blunders and dissipations must be entered into the account against it. Because of loneliness people have been driven into almost every kind of folly. Folk of all ages and circumstances can be afflicted by it. Yet, speaking generally, we do little about it and show scant concern for its sufferers.

\* \* \* \* \*

Let us first explore some of the facts. There are no figures to appeal to in connection with loneliness. In itself it cannot be standardised nor itemised. You cannot find a means of numbering the lonely. But there are statistics in connection with allied problems. I have stressed the links between loneliness and suicide. Some of the facts concerning the latter are open to examination. For instance we need to know that the world figure of suicides is set at more than one hundred thousand every year. In the United States it is said that it reaches something like 16,000 annually; and in the British Isles the rate is now in the region of 5,000 a year, with attempted suicides estimated at 30,000.[1] Each case represents stark tragedy, a life with its epitaph self-written, "Better dead".

It is not always easy to assess the reasons why people take this final step towards what they believe is self-annihilation. It can be said with certainty, however, that loneliness is often a part cause. Some other disappointment or tragedy may serve as the catalyst actually precipitating the attempt, but the action has had the day-in, day-out preparation of weeks and months of nagging loneliness. He was lonely—and last night his girl friend jilted him, or yesterday he heard that he was to be thrown out of employment: it is in some such fashion as this that the pattern is often worked out.

[1] *Ought Suicide to be a Crime?* Church Information Office, London, 1959.

Dr. Peter Sainsbury of the Maudsley Hospital carefully examined the cases of 409 suicides dealt with by the North London Coroner over a period of three years.[1] No less than 112 were of people who had been living alone, and in ten per cent of the cases it was explicitly stated—as in a note found after death—that loneliness was a dominant factor.

Miss M. von Anders interviewed a hundred people who had unsuccessfully attempted suicide. In setting out her conclusions after these psychological investigations she says, "A human being wants to exist for somebody and for something . . . he wants his achievement to be accepted and acknowledged . . . he wants his place to be defined by love and work."[2] When these conditions are lacking a person is living in real loneliness. Life loses its meaning: dazed and bewildered, the thought of self-extinction begins to loom in the mind.

Clearly, then, loneliness stands behind this problem of suicide, of whose size and importance we now know a great deal. The grey cloud casts a definite black shadow here.

\*     \*     \*     \*     \*

Another way of escape from loneliness is the flight into mental illness. By this method the self retreats from any feeling of responsibility. Notice: this evasion is not something *consciously* engineered, it is the *unconscious* mind that contrives this way out for the sufferer. It is a fact based on clinical experience that conditions of loneliness and the feeling that one no longer matters to anybody else can drive unstable personalities into such ways of seeming escape.

There are many other links between loneliness and mental illness. Since earliest times the effect of solitary confinement upon prisoners has been observed. This has often resulted in loss of reason, and—as has been rediscovered

[1] *Suicide in London* (London, 1955).
[2] *Suicide and the Meaning of Life* (London, 1947).

and re-emphasized in our own day—it is most powerful in breaking down morale and inducing what is now called "brain-washing".

An article in *The Times*[1] gave details of some experiments recently conducted in America and Britain in which a group of mentally and emotionally stable people were subjected to extreme forms of isolation. Three out of the fourteen American volunteers, who had been placed in a sound-proof room, with translucent plastic eyecups over their eyes, wearing earphones through which they were fed with "white noise"—an indeterminate sound cancelling out all extraneous recognizable sounds—could only endure it for fifty minutes, one-and-a-half hours, and three hours twenty minutes respectively. One of them declared, "Boy, you couldn't get me to stay any longer unless you held a gun over me." The thinking of those who endured the tests for any considerable period became disordered and in some cases disorganized. Here is scientific evidence corroborating what has always been surmised. Isolation and loneliness affect the powers of reason.

While the degree of effect of loneliness upon the total problem of mental ill-health is something no one can determine, we are again helped to recognize the size of the problem at which we are looking when we note that mental illness ranks No. 3 in the list of prevalent diseases in America, and that the latest British Health Department report states that nearly half the hospital beds in Britain are occupied by mental patients. No one can assess how many of these are mentally ill because of loneliness: but in a considerable number of instances it will have been a contributory factor. So behind yet another area of human suffering and misery we discern the outline of this same menace.

\*　　\*　　\*　　\*　　\*

[1] *Dangers of Loneliness: Some Experiences on Man in Isolation,* Jan. 15, 1960.

There is another facet requiring investigation. I was urgently reminded of this a day or two ago when talking to a sixty-year-old man who told me that no one could be lonelier than he. He was of the type to whom we now give the label "alcoholic". By this we mean people whose psychological make-up and physical frame have been conditioned over the years in such a way that they are now compulsive drinkers. Never again can they tread the path of moderation in this matter.

It was of the utmost significance that my visitor was willing to discuss his troubles. Ordinarily the alcoholic is psychologically withdrawn, unable to face his problems, and to acknowledge his defeat. The moment he is prepared to do this is for his friends a moment of hope. Behind the façade he has built up is, almost invariably, a strong sense of guilt. He has known what it is to have his erstwhile friends turn against him and find himself shunned because of his failures. In the first stages the alcoholic leaves his friends because he feels they resent his drinking; but in the later stages the matter is far worse. Now he does not want people to take any interest, or bother with him at all. One of the leaders of the Alcoholics Anonymous movement said to me, "Alcoholics are the loneliest people in the world."

What are the statistics covering this form of affliction? The answer is that the problem is sufficiently widespread and damaging that it is now a matter for the consideration of the World Health Organization.[1] In France and certain other countries it is a major problem. I quoted the report of the U.S. Department of Health as stating that mental illness was No. 3 in their list of major prevalent diseases. It may surprise many to know that No. 4 is alcoholism. Out of the three and a half million estimated alcoholics in the U.S.A., 900,000 are chronic cases. A conservative estimate of the latter in Britain would put this at

[1] See the pamphlet *Alcohol & Alcoholism* (Technical Report No. 94) published by the W.H.O. of the U.N. in 1955.

about a hundred thousand. What is much more alarming is that it has been reputably stated that six in every hundred drinkers in Britain become compulsive drinkers and are on the way to developing as chronics.

Here, then, is a special category of people becoming increasingly lonely. By the time they are confirmed alcoholics they suffer from what can only be described as a disease; and the full horror of this disease is that there is no cure.[1] This is another black shadow hanging over our civilization, big enough for us all to notice. Every one of the people listed as "alcoholic" can be added to any kind of computation of those in our society who are desperately lonely.

\* \* \* \* \*

When discussing loneliness it is the main features of the problem, however, that need to be kept in view. Only a fraction of lonely people are driven into mental illness, or ever contemplate suicide. And the number of alcoholics, though alarming, is not yet a high proportion of the total population. I have referred to these special problems because figures are available at these points. From them something of the magnitude of the problem can be gauged.

We need to be aware that many apparently simple facts concerning this subject merge into others that are anything but straightforward. They can neither be simply stated, nor easily solved. Especially is this so when loneliness is bound up with some form of neurosis. The late Karen Horney demonstrated that neurosis is the result of unresolved conflict in the personality, and declared that there are three

[1] The only way out is that of complete abstention. The movement called *Alcoholics Anonymous* has indicated the solution. Fundamentally it is religious: one must begin by admitting one's failure and then surrender the problem to a Higher Power who will take it over. The genius of the movement goes still further in inculcating a "day-at-a-time" philosophy, and in introducing the addict to what is often called group therapy. The alcoholic becomes part of a group practising this same spiritual programme. He can talk freely. The others know his difficulties from the inside. His loneliness vanishes in their company.

major ways in which people make an attempt to play off this inner struggle. They either became excessively amenable and compliant, or excessively aggressive, or preternaturally retiring. In other words, they either "move *towards* people", or "*against* them", or "*from* them". This is a most revealing analysis.[1]

Much conduct, therefore, that might look to the uninitiated like straightforward loneliness, Dr. Horney would have us see, really belongs to the third type of neurotic escapism. It is a "moving *from* people"—a neurotic compulsion towards isolation. In order to avoid the problems raised by too close contact with others, the defence-mechanism of one's inner nature adopts this strategy. Mrs. X will cross the road when she sees friends coming, and not know what has induced her to avoid them. Mr. A will manage to bring work home from the office so that he can avoid going out to the Joneses or having to accept an invitation to the club. He, too, will not realise his real reasons for so doing.

All of us in modern society, it is often said, are at some point of our nature slightly neurotic. That may well be. If a reader of this book who is lonely begins to wonder whether his state is a little more than the normal and is tending towards mental illness, the odd fact is that if he is asking questions at all, he can begin to feel reasonably safe. Neurotic conflicts are driven underground, and the genuine neurotic has rationalizations and excuses always ready to cover up his troubles. Neurotic conduct does not arrive fully grown, however, and it may be that many a possibility leading in that direction could be prevented by the straightforward looking at the problem which we undertake together in this book.

Should we discover, however, that the recommendations here made are consistently unacceptable and if indeed they cause something like a feeling of panic in our mind as we

[1] See, e.g., her book *Our Inner Conflicts* (Kegan Paul: London, 1946).

contemplate them, then our troubles are self-disclosed. What is outlined here will almost certainly be of too simple a character to deal adequately with our case. The personal care of some competent person—Christian minister or psychiatrist—is needed to unravel the complex situation in which we find ourselves. A neurosis is a form of illness requiring experienced guidance. These complex situations *can* be faced, and a real and satisfying solution found. To any such person I would say there is great help near at hand. Instead of running away from life, or trying to fight it, one can discover the way to live according to God's intention. "These conflicts *can* be resolved," said Karen Horney, "by changing the conditions within the personality that brought them into being. . . . I believe that man can change and go on changing as long as he lives."

\* \* \* \* \*

There is another fallacy to be avoided in connection with loneliness. It is to think that all people who are "geographically" alone are lonely in the sense in which we use the term in this book. Some people value privacy, and seem to thrive on it. While living isolated lives, the isolation is not always unwelcome. There is an amusing story of a woman living by herself who, after a B.B.C. Good Cause appeal, sent a donation to the National Old People's Welfare Council.[1] A dramatic reference had been made in the appeal to an elderly woman who died in a London flat, leaving behind a diary in which, for every day of the previous year, she had written the words, "No one came". The sender of the donation asserted her own point of view by writing, "From another old lady, who writes in her diary: 'No one came—thank goodness!'"

Living alone is, however, an outward circumstance which, for the reasons stated above, certainly encourages, if it does

[1] Mentioned in *Loneliness*, a pamphlet published by the National Council of Social Service.

not always lead to, seclusive habits and even to some degree of mental ill-health. This must be remembered in these days of increased single living. Let us look again at some of the figures: one and a half million people in Britain today are living alone—twice as many as in the early nineteen-thirties. This is quite a sizeable proportion of the population. As one radio commentator expressed it, modern life and economics tend to drive us into one-roomed burrows. This applies in many countries of the world.

The increased urbanization of modern society in itself encourages loneliness. Dr. Alan Walker in a survey of our basic problems[1] is certain that city life tends to develop conditions of loneliness in all sections of society, but particularly among the elderly. He quotes one lonely old lady, suffering from Paget's disease, whom he visited over a long period of years. "I'm not afraid of dying," she said quietly to him one day, "but I am afraid of living till I die." He also quotes a remark of Bishop Leslie Newbigin, "Modern cities have made people like grains of sand fretted by water from an ancient block of sandstone, ceaselessly churned around in the whirlpool of the metropolis as anonymous, replaceable units."

In this era we are growing a unique strata of older people. Because of the increased vulnerability of old age to loneliness this fact constitutes another special facet of this subject. Folk are living longer than they did. As the result of scientific discovery and increasing medical skill, this is becoming true throughout the world. It is especially noticeable in Britain and America. At the turn of the century in Britain, for example, one in twenty-one of the total population of 32,528,000 was 65 years of age or over. In 1954 one in nine was in that category, in a population of 44,274,000. The Government Actuary, in consultation with the Registrar General, has calculated that by 1975 the proportion of 65's and over will be one in seven. It

[1] *A New Mind for a New Age* (Abingdon, New York; Epworth, London).

means that within twenty years for every one hundred younger folk living in Britain there may well be twenty-three elderly people.

\*     \*     \*     \*     \*

New perils are forcing people into loneliness in some parts of the world today. In totalitarian countries men know what it is not to be able to speak freely. The fear of the informer drives many into acute spiritual isolation. They cannot share their innermost thoughts with others, and are denied fellowship at this vital point. One wonders whether the story told by Dr. Robert Jungk is entirely fanciful. It concerns an American scientist cut off from friends and relatives when critically ill and dying. This man passed away in hospital, alone, in case in his delirium he should mutter some atomic secret!

P. J. Bouman, a Professor of Sociology at Gronnigen University, believes that the history of the last fifty years is to be understood in terms of repercussions from loneliness. He entitles his study of these times *Revolution of the Lonely: a Mirror of an Epoch*.[1] Behind modern history he sees an underlying pattern driving leadership into ever lonelier positions and condemning man in the mass, through an increasing lack of spiritual values and a real sense of community, to progressively deeper isolation.

The wars of our generation, he would have us see, owe their origin to the striving after power of lonely men, driven by a nihilism that has issued in world-wide unrest. Their revolutionary aggressiveness has been answered and echoed in vast masses of people ready to have their inimical feelings externalised for them in this way. This social diagnosis is worthy of the closest study, and sets our concern about the problem against the greatest possible background. The real peril of our age, says Prof. Bouman, is

[1] Translated by Fernand G. Renier and Anne Cliff and published by McGraw-Hill Publishing Co. Ltd., New York & London.

found at this point. The nature of the cold war is here unmasked. It is an outworking from the basic loneliness of our times.[1]

The problem is indeed all about us. But the world-wide challenge cannot be taken up until loneliness is seen as something first to be tackled in the individual. We are dealing with something not to be remedied by governmental legislation, nor dosage with some universal drug. Large-scale palliatives will not help here. Of all the troubles flesh is heir to this is the one most needing individual treatment.

As a minister I have met a number of lonely people. They all needed specific, individual help. Each one required to be set right within himself and in terms of his own personal environment. This brings us, then, to the crux of our enquiry. We must look closely at ourselves and our children. For that reason we begin in the next chapter by looking at this problem in childhood. We leave the world of sociology and statistics behind and deal with our intimate human story.

[1] "The further the statesmen and politicians have diverged from the life of the people, the greater is their spiritual loneliness, the stronger their tendency to think along the lines of cold war formulas. The lonelier the masses they govern—masses on the way from being people's communities to being collective communities—the more the schematization of inimical feelings will find a response." *Revolution of the Lonely*, p. 408 (quoted by permission).

## Part I

# Loneliness in Life

*. . . I would like to point to the constant hazard which runs like a red thread through all the stages of development. It is the danger of loneliness and its consequences. The infant is lonely if he lacks tenderness and contact with the mother. The child is lonely if he lacks parental participation in play and conversation. The juvenile is lonely if he is rejected by his fellows. A more poignant loneliness comes during pre-adolescence with its intense need for intimacy with a single other person. Any companion is better than none, because loneliness is far worse than anxiety. We prefer to be tied to someone we hate than to be left in isolation. . . . The bitter fruit of loneliness is a distorted picture of oneself and therefore of other people; and the end is a warped person, incapable of living amicably with his fellows.*

JOHN COHEN

**2**

# The Lonely Child

*Most people, we suppose, must forget what they were like when they were children.*

FRANCIS THOMPSON

As soon as we begin to think back over our childhood, we can recall just how lonely a youngster can be. There were those night fears that kept us awake; those moments of terror in strange places when we lost contact with everybody we knew; and those times when, alone in the house, we wondered whether mother would ever return. . . . The sight of a terror-stricken youngster on the beach at the seaside, looking everywhere for parents and friends, reminds us of occasions, just as hopeless and terrible, when, years ago, we managed to lose ourselves in a crowd, and the whole world seemed empty. Fears, darkness, loneliness—yes, we knew it vividly then.

Some of us have reason to remember how cruel children can be to one another. The solitary, or the unusual, child is fair game for the others. They will bait him with fiendish maliciousness, if unchecked. As I write these words, my mind is busy not so much with memories of what I suffered in this way, as with what I and some others must have caused a small boy named MacDermott to endure. I often wonder what became of him. He was a frightened, lonely boy. For quite a time, I and the group with whom I shared the freedom of the London streets made life very much more miserable for him. I wish I could know that things had prospered with him since—and that he had forgiven us for our petty persecution.

If I had caused some other human being harm in this way, then the judgement of nemesis was waiting! Fortunate enough to secure a scholarship to Christ's Hospital at Horsham, I, as a young Londoner, found myself in an environment different from anything I had previously known. And as life went along in this new sphere, I came to understand for myself what loneliness and ostracism meant. A good deal of it, I do not doubt, was my own fault. But if anybody in a school develops disabilities or idiosyncrasies that mark him out from the rest, let him beware!

Looking back, I realise that it was years before I recovered from the effects of that experience at school. Unsure of myself and desperately shy, I went out into the world of business a lonely person. Bit by bit, I had to find release. It came, finally, with a new unfolding of life through meeting Christ, wonderfully and certainly, as the One who opens prison doors.

Generally speaking the troubles of childhood are sooner over and forgotten than those that come later. But it is also a fact that while they last they can cause as much— if not more—unhappiness. "The first realisation of misery," says Georges Bernanos, in his *Diary of a Country Priest*, "is fierce indeed. Blessed is he who has saved a child's heart from despair! It is a thing most people know so little about, or forget because it would frighten them too much." Of all the troubles a youngster endures, loneliness is one least easily brushed aside. The marks it makes are permanent.

We who are adults need to be more alert to the signs and signals of distress in children than we are. We can save them much unnecessary misery, and help them to prepare more satisfactorily for later life. If we fail to do this, the lonely child will inevitably find it more difficult later to enter into true relationships with others.

The small child's rightful endowment is happiness. One of the reasons why joy begins to fade all too quickly and "shades of the prison-house begin to close upon the growing boy", is that the love necessary for true growth may be denied him. This is the origin of so many psychological disturbances. If, for any reason, a child feels unwanted, the bright day is darkened, the developing intellect dulled, and from this time one will be able to trace the onset of apathy, slackness, insubordination, and even of delinquency.

Sometimes the trouble begins when a first child, having been the centre of parental affection, has to make way for a second who now seems to absorb all their attention. Sometimes a youngster realises from the beginning that he is not welcomed.

I heard recently of a middle-aged woman who all her life suffered from periods of depression. In these dark experiences her sense of isolation was so great that it was as if she were out in space alone, out of touch with everything. As a child she always felt lonely and was afflicted with nightmares. The fact is that she lived in an unhappy home, her parents eventually separating. Into the background of her life there was built the desperate fear of not being loved.

Is there any need in these days to underline the tragedy caused by broken homes? Children love both their parents, and want them together in a happy home. Tension between the adults has a powerful psychic repercussion on their children. If separation ensues, then going from one parent to the other makes for heartbreak. Living with one of them and not the other equally provides a dreadful psychological background. If the parents marry other partners, the state of affairs becomes almost intolerable. It is not for nothing that parents heading for matrimonial disaster are warned to remember the children. The effect of these separation situations is calamitous.

The great dread is that of being no longer wanted.

Dr. Leslie Weatherhead once spoke revealingly of a six-year-old daughter of missionary parents who, when they returned abroad, left her behind at boarding-school. Unfortunately, life in that school was hard. Still more unfortunately, the mistress with whom the girl was in continual contact took every opportunity to be difficult and even cruel. The girl lived for the day of her parents' return. In the meanwhile, a baby boy was born. When at last they met, the mother's first greeting to this little girl who had been marking off the days until she would see her parents was, "Why, I'd almost forgotten I'd got you." Thoughtless? Perhaps, after it was said, it was all the more criminal in that the mother failed to notice what harm her remark had caused. The girl grew up feeling rejected. So easily is the mischief done. A child wants to be loved and appreciated. The impulsion into loneliness starts when a child senses that no one really cares. Starved of affection, the hidden reaction of which Karen Horney wrote starts within the child, making normal relationships all the more difficult. It is the reaction of "moving away from people". One withdraws in order not to be hurt too easily again.

\* \* \* \* \*

For normal development, a child needs the environment of the home, with its give-and-take, and, especially, he needs a mother's tenderness. All this is familiar ground in child psychology. Some children, in this rough world, have, unfortunately, to grow up without their mother. Institutions that have to look after such children now go to great lengths to find the best substitutes possible for home and mother-love.

In a story from our own times Hugh l'Anson Fausset most beautifully and feelingly reveals the harm wrought by such deprivation. Ten days after he was born his mother died. His father, a Church of England clergyman, took this as a paralysing blow. Hugh thus not only lost his mother, but grew up with a father who, though keeping at his ministerial duties, harboured a grudge against God. With this eating at his heart and warping his nature, the father was no real help to his growing boy. "It is difficult," writes Hugh, "to imagine a home more inimical to healthy growth. The forces of death enveloped it and cast their shadow over the young life. And even as a boy of eight or nine I felt it in waves of desolation. Something that should be as natural an inheritance to the child as the sun and the wind was wanting. I did not know what it was. I only felt at times a void within that was unfulfilled, an ache that was unappeased. And lying awake at night I would long for a mother's kiss and a mother's immediate understanding. And sometimes I would close my eyes and fancy that I felt her breath upon my cheek."[1]

There was everything in that lonely home to make for an explosion—and it came. And everything was there, too, to make for the difficulties and disabilities in later life that Hugh describes, and which, equally frankly, he tells us were not overcome for a long time.

There are, of course, as many differences in the ranks of childhood as amongst grown-ups. Even within some families there are strange variations. Some children by nature are reserved and shy. Some have what are known as nervous dispositions. One cannot always alter these basic characteristics, nor would one wish to. But in assessing the troubles that any form of loneliness can bring we can see that it is the more sensitive type of child that suffers most.

Probably upon the shelves of a number of our modern youngsters there will be found a book or two bearing the name of Charlotte Yonge. It is interesting to find this Victorian novelist confessing that her trouble, when she was small, was night terrors. One nightmare that kept

[1] *A Modern Prelude* (Jonathan Cape, 1933) with grateful acknowledgement to Hugh l'Anson Fausset and the publishers.

recurring was that of being smothered "like the Princes in the Tower, or blown up with gunpowder" (the child of the mid-twentieth century doubtless translates these fears into things to do with H-bombs, flying-saucers, and Martians!). "In the daylight," she comments, "I knew it was nonsense. I would have spoken of it to no one, but the fears at night always came back." The way that children hug their secrets to themselves—even their secret fears—is proverbial. That, in itself, prevents adults from being able to help. This fact needs to be reckoned with in dealing with children.

When night fears are disclosed, parents can do a great deal. For one thing, they can be far more understanding if their children invent imaginary playmates to share their problems. For a time, this may provide a useful aid to a child conscious of loneliness.

Care and love, these are what children need. Their fears must be driven out by love. After the good-night kiss and the good-night prayer, the lingering presence of mother in the bedroom, busily tidying up, can mean much. For children the bedtime prayer should always be serene, happy, full of trust and faith. Prayers like this, bringing home the sense of God's nearness, form the finest antidote to loneliness then and all through life.

# 3
# Unwillingly to School

*At first the infant,*
*Mewling and puking in the nurse's arms.*
*And then the whining school-boy, with his satchel*
*And shining morning face, creeping like snail*
*Unwillingly to school.*

WILLIAM SHAKESPEARE

MOST youngsters enjoy their schooldays from the first, but there are some who for social, rather than for educational reasons have found them very difficult. For them it was a bewildering experience to be launched into this new world. I doubt if any experience faced as adults is ever likely to surpass that which confronts children leaving the shelter of home and mother for the first time, and plunging into this new environment. *We* know, of course, that there is nothing in the experience of which to be scared, but the child does not. Fortunately, there is far more understanding being shown at all levels today of what this stage involves.

James Kirkup, the modern poet, in *The Only Child*,[1] has given us a realistic account of what it meant to him. Those who have lived on Tyneside can easily picture the scene. It is a close community that lives in such places as Cockburn Street, South Shields, where James was born. The alleys and cobblestones of Tyneside in those days resounded with the cries and clatter of children who knew how to get a great deal of fun together. James tells us repeatedly that

[1] Published by Collins, in 1957.

31

though he was an only child he was not a lonely one. Even when he was "on his own" he was still not lonely. Then, as now, he says, he was perfectly happy in his own company: not lonely—until he went to school.

There came the day when his mother took him for a walk they had never taken before. It ended at the gates of Baring Street Infants' School. There she left him with knees knocking. He walked into the playground, swarming with youngsters, often looking back at the figure standing by the gate, waving and smiling bravely. Long afterwards his mother told him what that morning had meant to her. As for many a young mother, it was not only a lonely experience for her child, but a desolating one for her too. James Kirkup goes on to describe how that playground, and particularly the shed in the midst of it, into which on rainy days the whole school packed for shelter during playtime, became for him the pit of desolation. Silent and reserved as he found himself to be in this environment, the other children, and indeed some of his teachers, treated him, he says, as if he were an idiot.

Fortunately for so many modern children much of this agony is mitigated, if not completely avoided. They are profiting by the experiences suffered by past generations. What fine work, for instance, is done by Child Guidance clinics of the present day. How much misery is now short-circuited because both parents and children can receive expert advice in solving their problems.

An odd fact that emerges from these clinics is that what is coming to be called "school phobia" is increasing. When we were young a few of us were constitutionally averse to school, but the manifestation of this dislike in certain cases today is quite abnormal. Those concerned have to answer the question why it is that this phobia seems to be gaining ground. One thing is evident: initially it is due almost always to the fear of being separated from mother. "What will happen to her while I'm away at school?"—this is the sort of background fear disturbing the minds of small children. The difficulty is that of setting them at ease, and accustoming them to the fact that increasingly life will mean independence and separation from home.

Some children, like young James Kirkup, exhibit an emotional reaction to crowds. Child Guidance workers will tell you of youngsters found gasping and panting for breath in school assembly, or in the milling playground. Because of the presence of masses of misunderstanding children the basic sense of isolation is made the more dreadful.

Nail-biting, asthmatic troubles, eczema, stomach pains, headaches, twitchings and eneuresis—so many of these outward manifestations of distress are known to the child psychologist as symptoms of inward isolation and loneliness. The child who is slow at work and lacks confidence is often a child in whom this malady has set up barriers and difficulties. Those who are endeavouring to help the isolated child must encourage him to regain confidence. Often the trouble is that he thinks he has nothing to contribute, and that others are not interested in him. He must learn to give and take. When he dares to venture, the battle is half over.

At the moment there is much research into the effect upon infants of psychic shock and, particularly, that of separation from mother. To many people's astonishment the latter is now established as a factor of the greatest importance. We have quoted what Hugh l'Anson Fausset says concerning his own experiences. Modern psychology endorses his verdict concerning the profound effect that early separation can have. The first weeks of a child's life with its mother should be quiet and happy. If that period is anything other than tranquil and secure, it is likely to make for trouble later. So early does the problem of loneliness assert its importance.

Another factor, often overlooked, is the effect of bereavement on small children. We shall note this as one of the greatest causes of loneliness at all life's stages. The shock of this experience goes deepest in childhood. Daphne was a little three-year-old girl, vivacious and happy, whose father was her idol. Daphne had dancing feet. Her elder sister, laboriously learning at school, only had to show her intricate steps once and she had them. Then, unexpectedly and tragically, her beloved father died. It is two-and-a half years now since this tragedy. The once bright-eyed Daphne is no longer bright. She is one of the dullest and most lack-lustre children you could meet. She never dances now. The effect of this bereavement, at this early age, has been to make her a lonely and defeated soul.

When I was twelve, something happened to me the impact of which I can still feel today. It was something so unexpected, so unbelievable. On St. Matthew's Day, in September, the senior boys of Christ's Hospital come up to the City for a piece of pageantry and tradition which keeps alive the links between the school and the City of London. The first time I shared in this, I looked forward to it with the greatest eagerness. Part of the reason was that, so soon after the holidays, I would be able to see my parents and my two brothers for a few minutes. As we marched into the Mansion House, I scanned the crowd, but could not see them. Then I caught sight of my elder brother. He did not answer my smile.

Once inside, I noticed my home minister, Dr. Newton Flew, who happened to be an old boy of the school. He, too, looked very serious. As soon as we had filed before the Lord Mayor and, according to the ritual, had received a silver coin and shaken hands with him, Dr. Flew whisked me away, and took me to my brother.

"You've got to come home," my brother said. "Something's wrong." Then he had to tell me that Stanley, my younger brother, whom I had left only a few days before well and full of spirits, had met with an accident. Wearing a pair of roller skates, he had been knocked down by a lorry. At first my brother didn't reveal the whole truth, but as we neared home he managed to tell me that Stanley was dead. It was as if the bottom had fallen out of my life. I cannot even now describe how I felt.

When I got back to school some days later, I took up the reins, so I thought, where I had left off. It was then, however, that things really went awry. I hadn't the least understanding of what it was that was wrong. And, at the time, nobody else had either.

*　　*　　*　　*　　*

Have I made the point? Loneliness is not just an adult problem. All the things at which we shall look later are here in embryo in childhood. We begin to prove them at our mother's knee, and when we venture out to school. Loneliness is to be seen here, working its sinister way. And it must be tackled.

How can we help children in these matters, and discern the beginnings of trouble?

(1) The normal child is meant to be happy, living in a world full of interest and colour. If we meet a child with eyes glazed and dull, who is retreating from life instead of advancing to meet it, we have observed some of the outward danger signals, especially if we discover that the same child is spending restless nights. If he is out-at-elbows and ceaselessly awkward equally we need to take notice. It is for us now to win his confidence sufficiently to find out if some form of loneliness, fear or ostracism is causing the trouble.

(2) We must always remember about any child, our own, or in our charge, that though close to us, he does not in the full sense *belong* to us. He has his own life to live. We are there to help him find it and live it, to the full.

(3) He must therefore learn how to enter into good relationships with others. We must realise that we cannot make, or order, his friends for him. Nor can we, indeed,

35

force him to be friendly. But we can do much to foster right attitudes and provide the right opportunities. Above all he must learn to give and take. We can teach him to be thoughtful for others. A child not only needs to be loved but also to learn to love.

(4) We must be a friend ourselves to our growing children, making it possible for them to confide in us. In all these matters love is the key—not the love that makes an obvious parade of itself, but the love which acts as motive and driving force in all things: the love which is kind, but also firm. Love of this order is able to provide the necessary background of security whilst encouraging, as soon as is wise, the right kind of independence.

# 4

# Growing Up

*One other thing stirs me when I look back at my youthful days, viz. the fact that so many people gave me something or were something to me without knowing it.*

ALBERT SCHWEITZER

CHILDREN are seldom capable of analysing themselves. It is only rarely that the lonely child diagnoses his condition. But not so the adolescent. He knows what social isolation means and feels its sting. He has identified his trouble.

The stage he has reached may in itself help to drive him further into this state, for it often has an isolating effect. It is the "in-between stage", with the adolescent no longer a child nor fully adult. He is a:

> *Great big hobble-de-hoy*
> *Just betwixt a man and a boy.*

Of so much of the change going on within him he is only partly conscious: but he realises that a new driving force has arrived—that of powerful emotions concerned with the opposite sex. Because physical, mental and emotional developments are all proceeding at the same time, his feelings are more easily roused and more easily disturbed than at any other time in his life. A further hazard is that the rate of bodily change is not the same for everybody. He may, therefore, as contrasted with his compeers in these matters, find himself considerably in advance, or considerably lagging behind. We have noted how factors setting one apart from the group or accentuating peculiarities force children into positions of isolation. This tendency is aggravated in adolescence. Teenagers are hide-bound in their self-imposed conventions. They love to ridicule anyone not conforming to their standards.

In some cases the process goes further than ridicule. "An adolescent boy, particularly in the gang stage," says one expert, "delights in tormenting boys whom he does not like. A boy of foreign parentage, if his language, his clothes, or his actions be peculiar, is especially likely to be the victim."

When does adolescence begin? Some locate it as far back as twelve years of age. Certainly that may be so for a number of girls. But for boys it starts at about fourteen, lasting until eighteen or twenty, passing through one or two important phases.

If twelve is the recognised age, then some of the personal experiences recounted in the previous chapter belong here. The fact, however, is that my own adolescence was coloured by the experience to which I have alluded. Living in what some have called the monastery of a boys' school, I had been made to feel self-conscious even before the onset of the period notorious for aggravating that problem.

A number of us, boys and girls, can remember how real a problem our awkwardness and self-consciousness was at this time. Whenever I came home for the holidays and was invited to mix with other people, I felt nervous. This in-growing complex became so pronounced that my parents often had the greatest difficulty in dragging me to social events.

What caused me most confusion was an embarrassing habit of blushing. A boy at boarding-school knows purgatory if he finds his cheeks flushing and burning at inappropriate moments. The school chapel, where two sides of the school faced each other, was the worst place of all. I positively dreaded Sunday morning chapel, for there was one spot in the service during which I would have been happy for the floor to have opened and swallowed me. As we sang our way through the *Te Deum*, I knew that a certain verse was approaching. I suppose it was an index to peculiar adolescent troubles that it was the verse which announced that "He abhorred not the virgin's womb". I had not the slightest notion what it meant, except that it was something so essentially private and delicate that it seemed almost obscene to be chanting it out in the midst of eight hundred boys.

What troubles we create for ourselves! I imagine few will recognize anything of their experience in what I have just related. But I am sure not a few girls have passed through similar chronic phases of self-consciousness. In her book *Points for Parents*[1] Lady Pakenham pictures the troubles afflicting some of them at this half-way-house stage of life. Desperately coping with physical changes, they become preternaturally self-conscious, blushing at the least thing. The only solution some youngsters are able to find is either to avoid people altogether, or to cover up their confusion with a mad torrent of words. Lady Pakenham goes on to say that parents, in the main, fail far more often in sympathising with, and in understanding, their teenage children than the younger ones. "Fancy doing such a thing at your age—a great girl like you"—phrases like that spring to the lips, and betray our ignorance. Big they may be, these growing youngsters, but they are at the awkward stage, lacking in self-confidence and poise. They are already full of self-criticism, and do not need ours to add to the burden. Lady Pakenham is right when she says that the medium to help them is always love. It needs to be an understanding kind of love, based on knowledge as well as the desire to help.

[1] Based on a series of newspaper articles under that title, and published in 1954 by Weidenfield & Nicolson of London.

We have mentioned that with the bodily changes and sex-development of this period proceed deep psychological changes. Within growing youngsters there is a new instinct for independence and self-assertion which in itself can be most disconcerting. For this reason older folk often find them difficult to deal with, restless, impatient and self-opinionated.

Parents need to be prepared for this assertion of independence. Gradually and quietly, they should alter the tone of their conversation with their children. No longer should the parent talk down to the child, but, as far as possible, speak as one adult to another. Who has forgotten the thrill—and the encouragement—that one received when one of our parents talked to us, frankly and understandingly, as an equal? One grew inches. Documents such as Edmund Gosse's *Father and Son* reveal the tragedy that ensues when a parent at this stage endeavours to be repressive and distant. Parents need to understand what is their true relationship to their children.

*Your children are not your children.*
*They are the sons and daughters of Life's longing for itself.*
*They come through you but not from you,*
*And though they are with you yet they belong not to you.*

*You may give them your love but not your thoughts,*
*For they have their own thoughts.*
*You may house their bodies but not their souls,*
*For their souls dwell in the house of tomorrow, which you cannot visit, not even in your dreams . . .*

*You are the bows from which your children as living arrows are sent forth.*
*The archer sees the mark upon the path of the infinite, and He bends with His might that His arrows may go swift and far.*

*Let your bending in the Archer's hands be for gladness;*
*For even as He loves the arrow that flies, so He loves also*
    *the bow that is stable.*[1]

\*     \*     \*     \*     \*

In the developing phases of adolescence there are certain fairly well defined patterns of behaviour regarding friendships and social groupings. This is the time for hero-worshipping which results sometimes in an altogether foolish infatuation being lavished upon the one singled out for homage. In the early stage of adolescence girls tend to idolise one of their teachers, transferring this often extreme adulation, later, to some mature male who seems to be the embodiment of their dreams.

Strong friendships are made. Now the David and Jonathan relationship is often established. It is girls rather than boys, however, who during early adolescence most feel the need for a deep companionship. They look for someone who will be a confidant, sharing their trusted secrets. They want a "best friend" with whom to discuss their inmost thoughts.

Another facet of adolescent behaviour is the way youngsters organize themselves into fairly close groupings. The closeness of the group is again more noticeable among girls. At first these groups are of girls or boys unmixed. If a youngster moves into a new district, or changes school, it is very difficult to break into these sets. My wife told me of a girl who, at the age of fourteen, transferred to the school she was attending. The girl was brilliant and eventually, according to her school record, was due to become head girl. There were no peculiarities about her. Her sole offence was that she came into the school at the wrong time. The others just would not accept her; and because of her brilliance they were actively hostile

[1] Reprinted from *The Prophet* by Kahlil Gibran with permission of the publisher, Alfred A. Knopf, Inc. Copyright 1923 by Kahlil Gibran; renewal copyright 1951 by Administrators C.T.A. of Kahlil Gibran Estate, and Mary G. Gibran.

and jealous. Ultimately the headmistress advised her to leave! And this only because she was unacceptable to the rest.

The problem is not so acute for boys. If a boy possesses any kind of skill or flair, particularly in athletics, he can easily find his way into a new set.

"A loveless adolescent," wrote Dr. John Rathbone Oliver, "is bitterly lonely." He needs a friend. He needs a social group. If he is isolated and left out in the cold, everything about him will suffer. This is one of the main reasons why many leave school earlier than need be. It is not only the lure of wages that pulls. It is the hope of finding acceptability in another environment.

The adolescent has an intense desire to be acceptable and popular among his contemporaries. To girls this also means being considered attractive by boys. Some girls become most unhappy when they imagine they have not this physical quality. Impatient to attract the attention of the opposite sex, even at an early age of thirteen or fourteen, they do not understand why boys are repelled by their advances. Many become acutely miserable. Their unacknowledged fear is that it is due to their own lack of charm. When, later, they find themselves sitting out dances there is grave danger that a sense of inferiority will be confirmed and real loneliness begin.

Much of the tension in adolescence is lessened by daydreaming and indulging in fantasy. Sometimes quite extravagant attitudes are assumed—at least in imagination—in order to give relief, or to engender a sense of hope for the future which the harsh realities of life seem to have denied. Some adolescents, goaded by loneliness and a sense of inferiority, even begin to think of suicide. But, fortunately, it is largely a matter of thinking about it, or talking about it, and no more.

It is noteworthy that Phyllis Bottome, the psychological novelist and disciple of Adler, confesses that at the age of sixteen she had thoughts of suicide. No one who knew her later would have considered that such thoughts could have been serious.

Among some youngsters a feature of adolescent life concerns association in gangs. Now this form of teaming fits into the normal development of boys and girls from about eight or nine onwards, but usually ends at twelve or thirteen. The brightest and best adjusted adolescents, therefore, are not likely to join in this particular type of grouping. Others not so fortunate are drawn into it, almost willy-nilly.

It is nothing short of astonishing to discover the lengths to which this phenomenon goes. In New York and other American cities, it is said, gang-warfare between groups of adolescent boys is something of a nightly reality. Occasionally someone is killed. These gangs take to themselves high-sounding names such as the Bishops, the Jesters, the Hell-benders, ruling their ten-block territory under the dictatorship of a leader chosen for his bravado. Under this "president" there is a "war-councillor", responsible for the tactics of street battles, and a "gunsmith", who keeps in order the stock of flick-knives, guns, bicycle chains and other offensive weapons. This type of gang-warfare manifests itself from time to time in Britain.

Part of the explanation is to be found in the broken homes of the post-war era, in its cult of violence, and in the fact that so many of these youngsters were born amidst the insecurity of war. The lure of the gang itself is explicable in the dual difficulty raised by the emergence of the adolescent's awakening independence at the same time as he feels a deep sense of inferiority. The typical member of the "Jesters" and the "Bishops" will be illiterate and inarticulate, with no outlet for his emotions and ambitions. Concerning such youngsters the writer of a newspaper article says, "they are all over-compensating for a sense of inferiority and inadequacy—which would be unbearable if they had to endure it in isolation." The gang absorbs this, providing its members with a pseudo-bravado which individually none of them possesses. It is, in fact, a facet of loneliness that drives many youths into the gang.

Over the years I have spoken to young people, probation officers, police officers and youth organizers about this problem. One boy expressed himself in this way: "To go with others and sometimes do daring things, does something for you. It takes you out of yourself. You feel pretty small on your own, and you get kinda lonesome and bored. When you're out with the gang you can talk and think big. You're never lonely when you're with them."

"These boys are not really bad lads," said a police officer to me after a Teddy-boy rumpus in a London suburb, "at least—not most of them. Some of their leaders are using their courage and abilities in very strange ways, and sometimes they're downright vicious. But the bulk of them are just ordinary lads who in a few years will quieten down. They're restless and dissatisfied at home. This business of dressing up is all part of a struggle for self-assertion. Left alone, most of them would soon be all right. It's when they're ridiculed or their pride is hurt that you can look for trouble. You see," he continued, "it's a kind of inner loneliness that drives them together at this point in their development."

There is no doubt that Clubs and Youth Organizations fulfil in a positive way the function that the gang sometimes tragically affords for questing youth. Those who respond to the call for leadership in these clubs are affording a valuable service to the community, however little sung their praises may be. For many an impatient girl or boy new worlds have opened, tongues been loosened, new friends found, new ideas and interests discovered: concerts, theatres, tennis, badminton, youth-hostelling—self has been forgotten. Blessed are they who can introduce ingrowing youths to such outgoing interests!

\*     \*     \*     \*     \*

In the later stages of adolescence boy-and-girl friendships are to be expected. One psychologist says, "nothing that results from them could possibly be as serious as their failure to develop." What he is stressing is the *normality* of this phase. When this interest in the opposite sex is awakened parents again need to show the right kind of understanding. As to the manifestation itself they should neither foster nor retard it. "Calf-love" is intensely real. The last thing they should do is to make fun of these early relationships. In the later phase of adolescence the desire to love and be loved is strong. Unrequited love can, therefore, be a desolating experience.

But how can the lonely, inhibited youngster find his, or her way into satisfactory relationships? Dr. Robertson Nicoll, one-time Editor of the *British Weekly*, used to tell of a backward lover riding on top of an open bus with his girl. It was bitterly cold. The girl was despondent. "I feel blue," she said. "Nobody loves me and my hands are cold." "You shouldn't talk like that," answered the beau. "God loves you and your mother loves you, and you can sit on your hands." One must be a little more forthcoming than that if a youthful relationship is to flourish! Remember, a budding romance can be a beautiful thing if entered into lovingly, wisely and with grace—which means with the utmost consideration for all concerned. Some may, however, need the advice that came to one rather inhibited lover at a psychological moment. The girl lent him a magazine which had a page turned down at an article entitled, "Faint heart never won fair lady."

On the other hand, the lonely adolescent must equally beware of being cheated by the offer of a friendship or love that is not real. Lonely people are inclined to grasp at anything that is offered since it seems to afford a way out of their troubles.

What, then, are some of our conclusions concerning adolescence?

(1) It is often distinguished by awkwardness. For parents it can also be a distressing time. Something of the earlier lovable quality goes from their children. A new relationship has to be established. Many youngsters are not only physically awkward, but socially and mentally awkward, too. Because of this they come to be regarded as a liability, something of a nuisance. Parents may think their responsibilities are over by this time. They should think again. The right kind of help, shelter and partnership at this vital stage prevents the aggravation of difficulties faced by lonely youngsters.

(2) An adolescent is someone needing love. He or she needs, in turn, a close friend, access to the right social group, opportunities for friendship with the opposite sex, and, in due course, the reciprocated love of the right person. Deprived of any of these, loneliness with all its misery may result.

(3) It is important for school teachers to watch the formation of close groups, cliques or sets. They should endeavour to find ways of introducing newcomers to healthy social contacts in the new environment. Projects and activities extending across these group barriers should be encouraged. Extra-curricular activities are of great importance. At college and university there is usually more movement in and out of the community, and newcomers have a better chance of finding their niche. In America a considerable interest has been shown in this problem: social counselling has even been introduced into college life.

(4) Adolescents are devastating in their attitude towards others, criticising without mercy. The girls, especially, gossip endlessly. The lonely person will soon know in what category his colleagues have placed him. He must be prepared to struggle out of this, to nerve himself against rebuffs and to venture into social contacts in spite of the difficulties. He must also face himself as he really is, and

make terms with what he sees, prepared to be guided by this rather than by the dreams of his family and friends.

(5) Because the pressures towards standardization are so strong teenagers must not allow their own special gifts to be swamped or set aside. If they have something a little different from the ordinary to contribute, they must keep this alive at all costs! It is worth almost any sacrifice to preserve the creative element in human nature.

# 5

# Widening Horizons

> *... Till every moment as it flieth, crieth "Seize!*
> *Seize me ere I die! I am the Life of Life."*
> ROBERT BRIDGES

THE glory of adolescence is this: that amidst its storm
and stress the future is opening into the possibilities of
full maturity. For most youngsters it is a happy, developing, eager, wonderful time. One becomes aware of the
world and of the calls of the spiritual realm. The thoughts
of youth are long, long thoughts. One comes to despise the
mean and paltry and to fall in love with the great. This is
why youth's gaze on their elders—parents and teachers—
can often be so disconcerting. Theirs is such a crystal clear
way of looking.

It is thus that Jesus appeals now in something like the
fullness of His stature. In childhood He was admired as
Hero and Leader. Now He can be known as Friend and
Saviour, defeating the small and petty within us, and lift-
ing us to a fellowship with the greatness of God. When this
happens, then, at the centre of our nature, loneliness is
defeated. Through Him we have come into communion
with Love, and through this new relationship we discover
ourselves and other people. Walt Whitman asks:

> *Hast never come to thee an hour,*
> *A sudden gleam divine, precipitating, bursting all these*
> *    bubbles, fashions, wealth?*
> *These eager business aims—books, politics, art, amours,*
> *To utter nothingness?*

48

Have you known such an hour? Just recently I was turning the pages of an old diary which I started during my last school year. In it I chronicled some of my feelings at that time. It is strange to look across the years at one's young self. But here, in this diary, are the traces of one or two experiences that liberated me from the self-consciousness and self-centredness into which my private loneliness had forced me, bursting all these troublesome bubbles.

"I *must* like meeting people," says this callow youth to himself in one entry, "I must sympathise with them. I must get to understand other people." (He is on the right track when he is giving himself advice like that!) "I must like as many people as I can."

"I picture myself really alive on a great, wide plain," declares another page (here I was setting down, in semi-poetic vein, the yearning which at that time I felt so strongly towards a destiny then undisclosed) "full of singing voices; with a great wind blowing through hidden trees; above me the sky is full of stars, as of bright, twinkling eyes in heaven, watching and guarding me: but my great light, the star that I follow, is before me—sometimes burning steadily and sometimes flickering intermittently. What it is, I do not know, but I must follow it over the great mysterious, singing land, and then, when I get to journey's end, I shall find the light revealed and my guide waiting."

Now, this is not myself looking back and trying to re-create my adolescent feelings. Those words were written down *then*.

Did you, or do you, as a youngster, feel something of that sense of destiny ahead, beckoning, drawing? Notice the wide terms in which this particular youth saw his vision. I believe them to be typical of youth when the winds of God are stirring.

Not for a long time did I know what my great light was, the star that I would follow. But there came a day when that Light blazed in its fullness, and I knew that for me life would have to take a new course, and my self-absorption go completely. Then in truth those bubbles—fashions, wealth, those eager business aims, books, politics, art, amours— were reduced to utter nothingness when compared with what had now swum into my ken. Christ had come. Soon He beckoned. For me it meant ultimately taking the steps which led me into the ministry, and into my present sphere of happy service.

Youth is, thus, a time for idealism, for crusading. As the horizons widen one is ready to follow a leader whose eyes are also on the far distances.

How often has this spirit in youth been betrayed! Especially fatal is the call of false leadership and of false idealism sounding in the ears of youth previously starved of adventure. The tragedy is that the lonely and the frustrated consider it an inestimable privilege to be allowed to share in whatever crusade it is that beckons. Do you remember the reaction of William Wordsworth in the early days of the French Revolution? The wine of Liberty, Equality, and Fraternity went straight to his youthful head.

> *Bliss was it in that dawn to be alive*
> *But to be young was very heaven.*

Only later did he realise how his hopes had been betrayed. One of the pathetic things for us who now stand at some distance from the two great wars of our time is to turn back the records and hear youth—on both sides of the struggle—acclaiming the crusade. It is noteworthy that on our side there was not so much of this in 1939 as in 1914. Allied youth went into the Second World War much more open-eyed than did the generation of the previous war. We can recall the young Rupert Brooke, and marvel at what is before him as he writes:

> *Now God be thanked who matched us with this hour,*
> *And caught our youth, and wakened us from sleeping*

*With hand made sure, clear eye, and sharpened power,*
*To turn, as swimmers into cleanness leaping.*

The cleanness into which he leapt claimed his life and showed itself to be a foul, festering pool of iniquity before it vanished.

One of the merits of P. J. Bouman's book, *Revolution of the Lonely,* to which we have already referred, is that it tells its story and points its moral by presenting a series of kaleidoscopic flashes, showing people acting in a significant and representative manner at certain crucial times in our era. The reader is left to draw his own conclusions.

At one point we are given a glimpse of Adolf Hitler as a youth in Vienna, struggling in circumstances of poverty and degradation. Are we surprised at his reaction, now as a German citizen, when the 1914 war started and before him was the opportunity of fighting for the Fatherland?— "For me these hours came as a deliverance from the distress that had weighed upon me during the days of my youth. I am not ashamed to acknowledge today that I was carried away by the enthusiasm of the moment and that I sank down upon my knees and thanked Heaven out of the fullness of my heart for the favour of having been permitted to live in such a time."

Prof. Bouman also quotes Ernst Toller's entry in his diary: "How glad I am," wrote the poet, "that tomorrow I shall at last be able to join in the campaign. At last I shall be playing my part, proving with my life what I think and feel." It was after his return from the war that Toller came to write these so-different words: "More oppressive than the sharpest spikes of iron are the deeps of spiritual desolation and emptiness." [1] Hitler's disillusionment was allowed to work out in ways that led to further revolutionary ruin.

[1] The quotations are from *Revolution of the Lonely* pp. 171, 268, P. J. Bouman.

Bouman gives us glimpses of the Wandervögel movement in Germany, which started as an emancipation for
thousands of town-bred young Germans. They trekked
into the countryside, finding release and happiness. As
Nazism began to spread, it was an easy transition from
Wandervögel to Hitler Youth. The outward trappings of
the original movement were taken over—the brown shirts
and leather breeches, the camping and hiking, the singing
and guitar playing—and to its somewhat undefined idealism
were added the themes of power and glory. Under the
leadership of Baldar von Shirach the rambling changed
imperceptibly to marching, and the freedom of week-end
excursions gave way to the vast organised rallies of Hitler
Youth.

"It was no enthusiasm imposed from above," comments
P. J. Bouman, "that animated these marching lads. Their
enthusiasm sprang from gratitude at having been admitted
into a community, even if this community had all the stig-
mata of a dangerous uniform collectivity. They had
escaped from the chill of nullity and loneliness which had
driven the younger generation of the Weimar democracy
to despair. Beneath all the nihilism had lain the realization
that a life without ideals was hardly life at all. For the
first time, sacrifices were being demanded of them, and they
were ready to make the greatest of sacrifices, that of life
itself, if the Führer asked it of them. He who pledged
himself loyal to the Führer no longer stood lonely in life.
He was swept into the collectivism of the brown groups,
bound to others by new symbols, inspired by a new hope."[1]

Out of this recruitment, playing on the idealism of
youth, distorting it and twisting it, were fashioned the
fanatics who later marched half across Europe for Hitler,
and who manned his concentration camps and served his
gas-chambers. Ruthlessness had been proclaimed a virtue,
and mercy despised as a cult for weaklings.

[1] *Ibid* p. 335. Quoted by permission.

It is this same mixture of misplaced idealism, coupled with a sense of frustration and rebellion, that provides Communism with its recruits amongst the adolescents of the world. At the same time as one learns of universal brotherhood and the goal of "From each according to his ability and to each according to his need" one's inimical feelings are provided with objects for hatred and attack. One is told that to defeat the enemies of world Communism is to hasten the revolution and advance the course of history. Against these enemies, any weapons are lawful. And in all this one's personal sense of insignificance is lost. One is welcomed into a mass movement providing a goal and a purpose.

How desperate is the need for youth to find a fitting answer to its frustrations and a fitting object for its idealism. One of the lessons of our era is that dictators and revolutionaries have found the powder magazine they require every time amongst the frustrated adolescents in the community. Hungry for leadership, and burning for some outlet for their innate idealism, they have been employed over and over again as the stooges and dupes of the would-be dictator.

The world is in crying need for the right sort of crusading! Somehow good causes must be presented with greater liveliness and power. Truth must be seen to glow with fiercer light than falsehood. Youth is prepared to sacrifice and if need be to suffer in a cause that has flame and fire. It will not give its allegiance to colourless entities.

The reason why some churches lose their young people at this adolescent stage is that there is no drama, no appeal, no challenge about church life at the very time when youth is yearning for these things.

A bolder and, in the end, a safer strategy is needed. Youth's crusading zeal must be allowed its outlet. It provides the energy that both the Church and the world continually need renewed. We must also find ways and means to prevent the lonely and unsatisfied in the ranks of youth from falling prey to those who will use their zeal and keenness for wrong purposes.

Above all it is important that youth should learn of the Young Man who, years ago, gathered around Him a band of dedicated young people some of whom later were to justify their promise that they would die for Him. There is no other cause like His, nor any other leader fit to approach Him. No one who follows Him is led into a blind alley. The ways open out, always, into the ever-widening horizons of eternal life.

So it is that what we shall say later concerning the defeat of loneliness also applies to questing youth. Multitudes of young people, struggling into maturity, need above all else to establish true relationship with others. Let them determine to do this, and to take all the steps shown to be needful. At all costs they must find the way into the full life that is God's intention for them.

**6**

# For Better, For Worse

*Human beings do not go hand in hand the whole stretch of the way. There is a virgin forest in each; a snowfield where even the print of birds' feet is unknown.*

VIRGINIA WOOLF

AFTER the death of George Crabbe, one of his children, rummaging among his personal effects, found a piece of paper out of which fell an old, worn wedding-ring. It was the ring the poet had given his wife years before, and since her death had kept wrapped in a piece of paper on which were written the words:

> *The ring so worn as you behold,*
> *So thin, so pale, is yet of gold;*
> *The passion such it was to prove,*
> *Worn with life's cares, love yet was love.*

In the floodtide of youthful attraction, two people joyously enter matrimony. This is the stage which is always the climax of fairy stories—"and so they married and lived happily ever after". In reality, as many of us know, it is but the beginning of a relationship which, with its ups and downs, its testings and adjustments, carries us through to ever new understandings of what love really means.

Mark Twain wrote a revealing letter to his fiancée two months before marriage. It reads, "We shall never be separated on earth, let us pray we may not be in heaven. Our wedding day will be the mightiest day in the history of our lives, and the holiest, for it makes of two fractional lives a whole: it gives a new revelation to love, a new depth to sorrow, a new impulse to worship."

Our Lord saw marriage as a God-ordained partnership that uniquely makes the partners one, and He quoted with approbation (Matthew 19: 5) the Genesis text which refers to this on the physical level. It is God's intention that man and woman should come together in such a relationship that, on all levels, they should be united in bonds of the greatest intimacy.

It is not surprising, therefore, that when one turns to statistics and social surveys, loneliness and resulting diseases are not so evident among married people. It afflicts the unmarried, the widowed or the divorced much more. There are, for instance, among the two hundred case histories at the beginning of Rowntree and Lavers *English Life and Leisure* ten which mention loneliness. Of these ten only three concern married people, and in each instance the word "married" should be in inverted commas, for they serve but to emphasise the point we are making. There was no true marriage.

We have spoken, also, of the close association between loneliness and mental ill-health. The County Medical Officer of Health for the London County Council reporting for the year 1956 states that mental welfare officers dealt with a much lower rate of married than of single, widowed, or divorced persons. The difference is all the more striking because approximately one-sixth of the married people seen by the mental welfare officers were in fact separated, but for statistical purposes had to be included in the married group. The figures are interesting and speak for themselves:

| Single | | Married | | Widowed | | Divorced | |
|---|---|---|---|---|---|---|---|
| Male | Female | M. | F. | M. | F. | M. | F. |
| 37.2 | 33.7 | 16.5 | 21.9 | 58.9 | 54.3 | 54.1 | 51.2 |

Man is made for intimate social relationships; in the family and in a home he is at his best. A remark of Monsieur André Maurois, the French writer, is relevant. Said he: "I do not think that a Head of State or a leading figure in the arts can know real happiness unless there is one person beside him with whom he can remove his mask. . . . 'One feels so alone,' a famous man, around whom a little court revolved, once told me. Love, whether of children, wife or friends, breaks the prison of loneliness."[1]

While a happy marriage is a relationship from which loneliness is excluded, provisos must be made and caveats entered. I knew a couple who married, deeply in love; but within a few weeks the girl had run home to mother. The latter had brought up a large family, upon whom she had lavished care and affection. Though very much in love, living alone with her very quiet husband was such a lonely experience that the daughter could not bear it. "The house seemed so dead," she said, "with just the two of us after the eight or nine I'd been used to." Fortunately the husband was an understanding person. The mother bought a larger house and he and his wife moved into some rooms there. It proved to be an ideal solution in their particular case—though it would be anything but that in others. The woman became ecstatically happy, with her husband, and with her own family in the background.

A contributor to the controversial B.M.A. 1959 publication, *Getting Married*, says, "Probably the last thing any of us expects to feel when we get married is lonely! We know that it can happen to elderly folk, or to mothers whose families have grown up and left home. But surely not to anyone young, and newly married? Maybe it is this very fact that makes the situation a little baffling.

---

[1] Quoted from pp. 164 f. of *To The Fair Unknown*, by permission of the publishers in Britain, The Bodley Head. American rights held by E. P. Dutton & Co. of New York.

But, for the wife who has given up her work on marriage, the day can seem very long and very lonely. She may find herself suddenly transplanted to a new district miles away from all her friends and even her family. Her new home may be in a part of the country that is newly developed but still unorganised."[1] The article continues by using this as a text for a sermon on getting to know one's neighbours, and on joining women's organisations such as the Women's Institute or the Townswomen's Guild: all of which is excellent advice.

Also, let newly-weds moving to a new area remember to seek the right church, see to the transferring of their membership and share in the new church's worship and activities. Let the lonely wife join the Young Wives' Circle, and lose no time in doing so.

There is a later period, too, when the woman in the home may begin to find time hanging heavily on her hands. The day comes when the children grow up, finding an independence of their own. Moving to a small house or flat is not necessarily the answer to the new situation, for its very size prevents visitors from coming to stay and it can become a prison. And some women—often for want of something better to do—spend most of their time polishing the bars of their prison and, because of excessive house-pride, make the home even more uncomfortable for their husbands!

It is the womenfolk who experience *these* aspects of loneliness in marriage. In many cases the situation is aggravated by the way they are left by themselves for longer periods than is either right or wise. A little while ago I heard a report of a new scheme of mental-health-visiting inaugurated in the Worthing area, on the South coast of Britain. One observation was very revealing. When finances permit many people, in love with the country and sea, move to the coast. In Worthing, apparently, many women have

[1] Quoted by kind permission.

paid a peculiar penalty for this. Husbands working in London need much more travelling time for their daily journey. The resulting extra loneliness, said the report, has caused some women additional mental stress.

Hepzibah Menuhin was talking recently on the radio. This talented woman, herself a famous musician and sister to the still more famous Yehudi Menuhin, not only runs an efficient home but is also actively engaged in much social work. She was speaking as someone transplanted into English society, having lived in America, with a number of worldwide contacts. Hepzibah Menuhin believes English women are left far too much on their own—and she is not referring just to the separation due to daily work. In Britain, she notes, there is a traditionally male society. The home is organized round the husband, and he—without thinking about it—assumes he is entitled to use the home and grace it when he thinks fit. Men seem, indeed, to leave it on every possible occasion, in the evening as well as the day. Off they go to their sport, or to the club, and the wife is left unnecessarily and sometimes dangerously alone. The failure to continue to seek her company must be all the more baffling to many a wife herself since it is such a reversal of what happened during courtship. Then the poor man could not see enough of the beloved. Now, it would seem, the problem is how to see her as little as possible!

But it must not be thought that this particular danger in domestic life is one which affects only the woman. Many a man has felt cold-shouldered out of his home when the children arrive. It is usually done unconsciously, but some women become so absorbed in their children that they seem to have no time to continue with their husbands the camaraderie of earlier days. As some women have discovered to their sorrow, lonely men sometimes seek satisfaction elsewhere. It is possible in this way for one or other of the partners in marriage to experience a real sense of loneliness. What both partners must guard against is indifference.

We have said that loneliness is something known more by the single, widowed, or divorced person than by the married. Not often does a divorcee, or someone separated, give us a picture of what the new life of separation entails. The Duchess of Windsor writes most revealingly of this. At the age of twenty she married an aviator in the United States Navy, knowing little about him or about the rocks and shoals of matrimony. Her husband was addicted to drinking which, she says, intensified a "jealous and sadistic streak" in him. Life was made unbearable. Slights and insults were even extended to her in public, and after five-and-a-half-years they parted.

Concerning this time she confesses: "Loneliness descended upon my spirit, an emptiness I had not counted upon. A marriage, even one that goes awry, generates claims and needs that persist like an afterglow long after the emotional fire is burnt out. The mind and the heart continue to remember the happy and cosy times together, and the unpleasantnesses recede. Now, having separated —as far as I could tell for ever—I began to learn that a marriage is not so easily uprooted, that divorce is no escape. There is no evading what has been lived through together. . . . The real essence of any marriage that has struggled, however unsuccessfully, towards happiness, lies in the growth of a wordless understanding that what is acceptable to one partner will be acceptable to the other. Between the storms, Win and I had known briefly a sharing of this kind. And the habit of shared experiences makes the process of detachment inexpressibly difficult. There can be no summary and dramatic end to a marriage —only a slow and painful unravelling of a tangled skein of thread too stubborn to be broken."[1]

[1] Quoted from *The Heart has its Reasons* by permission of Michael Joseph Ltd.

The widow, or the widower, feels this in an even deeper way for there has been no desire for separation. In this dark situation one feels that one's heart is gone. At such an hour it is the quintessence of loneliness that is felt, and it represents a great test. I have seen a fine man, a fine woman, go completely to pieces at such a time. Later I shall write more fully concerning the experience of bereavement in general.

\* \* \* \* \*

It is not for nothing that literature is full of the eternal triangle. Once again it is often loneliness within marriage that impels a married person into this disaster. The best advice to anyone faced with this kind of domestic situation is to end it, and be quite ruthless about it, if need be. Prevent it from developing at all costs. And beware the subtle snare of calling the association mere platonic friendship. The full love which is what we think of in connection with marriage can properly be given only to *one* other person.

There is a further warning of which husband and wife should be aware: what is sometimes mistaken as loneliness within marriage is not that at all. Rather is it a reminder that all of us human beings, however close our relationship, sometimes need a little distance between us. The soul must keep its own integrity and inviolability. Every individual must safeguard a certain essential privacy.

Perhaps we have been searching for a satisfaction in a human being which we can find in God alone. He is our soul's final rest, and all our relationships are fulfilled only when related to Him. "Thou shalt have none other Gods before me." It is possible for us, sometimes, to make an idol of another person. Never must anybody be put in *His* place. "Whoso gives God a secondary place," said Ruskin, "gives Him no place at all." He must be first.

Then all other relationships fall into their rightful position. "Seek ye *first* the Kingdom of God and His righteousness, and all these things shall be added unto you," said Jesus.

> *When, with all the loved around thee,*
> *Still thy heart says, 'I am lonely',*
> *It is well; the truth hath found thee.*
> *Rest is with the Father only.*[1]

In a previous chapter I quoted from *The Prophet* by Kahlil Gibran. There is another poem in that collection in which Almitra asks the master concerning marriage. He answers:

> *You were born together, and together you shall be for evermore.*
> *You shall be together when the white wings of death scatter your days.*
> *Aye, you shall be together even in the silent memory of God.*
> *But let there be spaces in your togetherness.*
> *And let the winds of heaven dance between you.*
>
> *Love one another, but make not a bond of love:*
> *Let it rather be a moving sea between the shores of your souls.*
> *Fill each other's cup but drink not from one cup.*
> *Give one another of your bread but eat not from the same loaf.*
> *Sing and dance together and be joyous, but let each of you be alone,*
> *Even as the strings of a lute are alone though they quiver with the same music.*

[1] George Macdonald, *To One Unsatisfied*, quoted from *Gathered Grace*, by permission of the publishers, W. Heffer & Sons of Cambridge. There is another of his short poems whose title is much longer than the two words of the "poem", *The Shortest and Sweetest of Songs:*
Come
Home.

*Give your hearts, but not into each other's keeping.*
*For only the hand of Life can contain your hearts.*
*And stand together yet not too near together:*
*For the pillars of a temple stand apart,*
*And the oak tree and the cypress grow not in each other's*
  *shadow.*[1]

My wife reminds me of something I said to her over a cup of tea on our second outing together: "It is very important that married people should be companions as well as lovers." I must have possessed more wisdom then than I knew, for all our days together since have proved the truth of that statement. There needs to be, in a happy and lasting marriage, a fundamental area of mutual interest and agreement, based on an undergirding heart-fellowship.

In those spartan days in which I grew up, a Methodist minister was not allowed to marry during the seven years of his probation. My wife and I were engaged for six long years. Too long? Well, we certainly felt so then, but that long engagement assured us of one thing: that by the time of our wedding we already knew one another extremely well. Young people need to have a fairly long period of courtship, much longer than most allow themselves today. During courtship they should determine if they are temperamentally and intellectually suited, whether they have common standards of morals, the same type of humour, and whether they agree about religion. All these levels of agreement are necessary if there is to be no vital division and loneliness later. The idea of the attraction of opposites can be most misleading. There is, of course, a great truth in it, but the differences between partners in marriage need to be complementary, not contradictory.

[1] Reprinted from *The Prophet* by Kahlil Gibran with permission of the publisher, Alfred A. Knopf, Inc. Copyright 1923 by Kahlil Gibran; renewal copyright by Administrators C.T.A. of Kahlil Gibran Estate and Mary G. Gibran.

# 7

# Defeating Unfulfilment

*Whoever you are! claim your own at any hazard!*
WALT WHITMAN

ANOTHER frequent source of loneliness is what might
be described as unfulfilment. Most of us are fortunate in having satisfying work and happy relationships
—those of home, friendship and marriage. For some, however, these things do not develop. The normal, or the long
desired, is either impossible or its fulfilment frustrated.

A friend of mine lives in a hostel which has as its goal
the helping of men who are homeless and who, for some
reason, have lost their way in life. It has a splendid record.
After a spell of living there many find their feet again.
"Tell me," I asked my friend, "are any of the men at
Western Lodge lonely?" A somewhat rueful smile crossed
his features. "You know," he said, "we're all lonely people
here." Living together in a hostel, however well run, is not
the same thing as living in a family.

Cyril Garbett, recently Archbishop of York, had the
reputation of being an austere man, somewhat difficult to
deal with. For years, so his biographer tells us,[1] he kept
in the top drawer of his desk a small rubber ball which had
belonged to a boy called John Hooper. Garbett had never
married but he always loved children and got on easy terms
with them. John Hooper was the son of his chaplain. He
died when quite small. Maybe that souvenir kept in so

---

[1] *Cyril Forster Garbett, Archbishop of York* by Canon Charles Smyth.

prominent a place tells us much concerning the late Archbishop of York. "Maybe," says one commentator, "Garbett was hard just because he was lonely."

Ever since I began to think in terms of the Christian ministry, one of my heroes has been Phillips Brooks, the American Bishop of whom it was said that when he came out into Newspaper Row in Boston the sun came out, too! Because of my interest in him, I have carried round, during my itinerancy as a Methodist minister, the large two-volumed Life written in 1900 by Alexander V. S. Allen. In the second volume (what monumental books used to be written in those days!) there is an illuminating entry. To all outward appearance, the career of Phillips Brooks was an uninterrupted success story. His characteristic, as the Newspaper Row reference itself suggests, was a perennial sunniness of disposition. He himself claimed that his life was one of great happiness. Yet, after the death of his mother in his later years, we are told that a sense of loneliness, which had always been nagging at him, deepened.

His biographer writes, "He began to realise how the course of his life condemned him to increasing loneliness for the remainder of his days. He yearned and hungered for human affection. . . . To Bishop McVickar he admitted that it was the mistake of his life not to have married. Sometimes, in the happy homes of his younger friends, he seemed to resent their happiness, as though they taunted him in his greatness with the inability he had shown for human love. More than once he is known to have said, 'The trouble with you married men is that you think no-one has been in love but yourselves. I know what love is: I have been in love myself.'"

Bachelordom is sometimes a self-chosen course of life; but spinsterdom rarely so. There can be no question that among the loneliest people in our society are the folk referred to sometimes as old maids and spinsters. How bravely many of them face the increasing loneliness to which their unmarried state dooms them! How splendidly many of them achieve what the psychologists used to call a sublimation, pouring their gifts of character and love in one form or other into the service of the community.

It should never be forgotten that many of the older members of this group lost their fiancés in the First World War, and that the Second World War brought a new group of spinsters into being. These were folk eagerly looking forward to marriage. How sympathetic and understanding the rest of us ought to be.

There was a Miss E. whom I knew in the 1930's in Manchester. No bitterer blow could have come her way than the news that her fiancé had been killed—in the battle of the Somme. They had been devotedly in love. Quietly and steadily, Miss E. found ways to assuage her grief. She was always the first to comfort others who had similar news to bear. She began conducting classes in elocution, a subject in which she had some proficiency, and was especially keen to teach in Girls' Clubs and other organisations that needed voluntary assistance. In this and other ways she achieved something of a sublimation. Her people were wealthy. She was generous to good causes. When the war was over she used to travel abroad with some of her friends. And yet . . . there was always an unfulfilled ache, a yearning unsatisfied, a wound never properly healed. She could not bear to listen to references to the "young men who gave their lives". At such times her control broke down, and tears came unbidden.

It must never be assumed, however, that the path of fulfilment for every man and woman is meant to be that of marriage. This plainly is not the case. There are some not meant to work in double harness. Their destiny, and even their disposition, takes them in another direction. Clearly, they have a vocation to stay single. Serious trouble has overtaken people who have rushed into marriage ill advisedly, or who married against their better judgement. Dr. Hadfield, the psychologist, once declared that half his women patients came to him because they were married, and the other half because they were not!

One of the frustrations that can arise within marriage and cause great loneliness—and this applies especially to women—is an unfulfilled longing for children. Many couples look forward to this blessing. The years go by, and their hopes are denied, or perhaps a child is born only to die in early childhood and the parents are told that they should not have another. We are living in days when no married people should experience frustrations of this kind without obtaining the best medical advice. Nor should they fail to seek deeper help and guidance. It is quite remarkable what quiet faith and prayer can achieve in these realms.

I knew of a couple—the husband was a minister—who looked forward eagerly to having a family. But it did not happen so. Eventually they sought expert advice. The wife was told that she could not expect to bear children: why not think of adoption? They had thought of it, a very great deal, and were prepared to open their home and lavish their love upon a little one, if this expedient were the only way. So, after praying and asking God's guidance, a boy, aged a few weeks, came into their home. The mother found a new bliss in caring for him. And then, the impossible happened. The explanation, I suppose, would be that the caring for this little one, the awakening of all the maternal instincts, unlocked something in the mother. Within a year she had a baby of her own. She has had another since. And those three children are growing up, all of them dearly loved.

\*     \*     \*     \*     \*

There are other kinds of frustration that can lead to loneliness. The crippled and the handicapped know something of this: the folk of whom Helen Keller is not only the perfect example, but for whom she is also the shining exemplar. She shows how these handicaps can be overcome and loneliness defeated. How cut off she could have been! Unable to see or hear, what chance had she of communicating with others? But Helen was a girl with grit, and she was fortunate in finding a teacher who really cared. Patiently and understandingly, Miss Sullivan evolved a sign language by means of which Helen, through the medium of pressures on the palm of her hand, could understand what she said. Eventually, deaf Helen learned to speak. The story of how she went to the university, took her examinations, became a world figure, having written, lectured, and appeared in films and television, is one of the epics of our time. Here were all the possibilities of a life cut off, becoming completely in-growing, yet Helen and her friend circumvented this.

What should be done by anyone faced with conditions of unfulfilment? Helen's story suggests the answer. One should always try to work towards the ordinary goals and satisfactions. As far as is possible handicapped people should think of themselves as normal and others should treat them so. Nothing exasperates blind or crippled folk so much as being dealt with as if they were abnormal. I remember a blind person saying to a group of sighted people, "You know, we're exactly the same as you—except that we can't see." Precisely! That is it . . . "except that we can't see." We must not let that fact so colour our relationship that it obliterates everything else. The things that we share on the ordinary human level are far greater than this one point of difference.

Rolf Thomassen's life story, a best-seller in Norway, has recently been translated into English under the title *Beyond Today*. It is the record of a boy "not like others"— as he repeatedly overheard people saying of him. Born a spastic, this lad longed for normality and for the exercise of the creative gifts stirring within him.

Rolf's trouble meant that he had no control over his limbs, and that he was unable to walk or hold anything in his hands. When in the company of other people he would be betrayed into convulsive movements and shudderings, and to a further clouding of his incoherent speech. By dint of heroic effort he learnt to paint by holding a brush in his teeth. Some of the music in his soul found an outlet through learning to play the zither similarly. Many of his paintings, by the sale of which he now lives, have won acceptance, and this not because of their unusual origin but because of their intrinsic merit.

Eventually this crippled man became able to operate an electric typewriter, by the method of touching the keys with a stick attached to his chin, and wrote his auto-biography.

What sustained him and gave him courage was a strong Christian faith. This released him from loneliness and enabled him to conquer his disabilities. Repeatedly, he says, he has proved the truth of the Psalmist's words, "By my God have I leaped over a wall."

It is part of the story, too, that Thomassen has had much to do with the formation and the running of Disabled Homes and Clubs in his native Norway. To his surprise, when he first started mixing with his fellow sufferers, instead of finding an aggravation of his difficulties, he found release and fellowship. "Like many others," he writes, "I had wrong ideas with regard to disabled folks and their movement. . . . When I saw all the disabled people gathered together, I lost heart and thought: now the tragedy will begin. For there they were in wheel chairs, on crutches and sticks and other aids. . . . I almost shuddered at the thought of having to be with these people for three whole days. However, I was soon to change my opinion, and before long thought them to be the grandest people I had ever met. The more we talked together, the more we forgot wheel chairs, crutches and sticks."[1]

Whatever it is in us that yearns for fulfilment should be constructively and positively channelled into achievement benefiting both others and ourselves. There are those who have seized the very thing that frustrated them and turned it from a handicap into a new and glorious opportunity for service. Louis Braille, afflicted with blindness, became an organist and an educator. He used his handicap to such effect that he evolved the Braille script so that the blind can read!

A supreme example of tragedy turned to triumph is surely that of Josephine Butler, whose four-year-old daughter, coming out on to the upstairs landing to greet her, plunged to death in the well of the staircase. Out of her grief for the loss of her child, Josephine Butler rose to do work without parallel for children. Catherine Marshall, after experiencing first something like exaltation after the death of her husband, came to know fierce loneliness. Out of this she climbed by writing of him. And this she did in such a way that her books have become an inspiration to thousands. In the very grasping of the nettle a new kind of victory is won.

\* \* \* \* \*

One must be certain, however, that in working out a new goal one is not, in fact, running away from the direct challenge. Modern psychologists and physicians speak most revealingly of the death-wish. All is over with a patient if he resigns himself to death. In the path of unfulfilment the way is to accept what is there courageously and realistically, not to run away. Facing grief or disaster bravely can bring release and ultimate victory. We need to find some

[1] *Beyond Today*, pp. 57, 59, Rolf Thomassen, tr. by Torgrim and Linda Hannaas (Robert Hale, London, and Augsburg Publishing House, Minneapolis, Minnesota, U.S.A., copyright owners of the translation).

way over and through the experience—through to the other side! There is *always* such a way, with God.

There are people who have renounced what others would regard as fulfilment for a greater love's sake. Our Lord in Matthew 19: 11 f speaks of this. We have had, and still have, bachelor leaders, unmarried priests, deaconesses, nurses, nuns, etc., free in their obligations and responsibilities as married people are not. But, again, one who is thinking of undertaking some such voluntary sacrifice must be sure that it *is* for a greater love's sake: then, and only then, will the greater swallow up the less. The headmistress of a girls' school whom I know sometimes tells her senior girls of her own experience. She refused marriage for the sake of an academic career. Now, though she has been most successful, she knows she made a mistake.

Evangeline Booth, that colourful figure who followed in her grandfather's footsteps to become General of the Salvation Army, once said: "My only real love wanted me to give up the Army. So we parted. Instead I have been devoted to millions instead of one. I am not sorry; but I do remember."

Unfulfilment, of whatever character, is a "thorn in the flesh", valueless and useless, destructive, cutting us off from life, until accepted and grafted into our being, to result in some new growth. Happy are they who, having prayed about it, discover these new possibilities. "My grace is sufficient for thee," said the Lord to His apostle facing a frustrating circumstance, the nature of which we shall never fully know. With our co-operation God is able to lead us to fulfilment by a way we have not seen.

No longer is there handicap, but achievement! And the wonder of it, and the glory of it we gladly ascribe to God, as we are privileged to serve in His Kingdom.

# 8

# The Dark Wood

*"When I'm alone"—the words tripped off his tongue*
*As though to be alone were nothing strange.*
*"When I was young," he said, "when I was young . . .*
*I thought of age, and loneliness and change. . . ."*

SIEGFRIED SASSOON.

DANTE begins what some have claimed to be one of the world's finest poems with the words:

*At the mid-point of my life*
*I came to the dark wood. . . .*

At this "mid-point", Dante had to go through Hell and Purgatory, and Paradise, before he was able to find the way.

It is strange how often we meet with this symbolism of the dark wood in connection with this stage of life's journey. Hugh Walpole, telling the story of the downfall of Archdeacon Brandon,[1] notes the time when life changed for this once immaculate, superior being. It was in mid-career, when his son was sent down from Oxford. Things were never the same after that. To underline the significance of what was happening, Hugh Walpole recalls an old German tale. A traveller is undertaking a journey to a certain castle. He is told that all will be well until he comes to a wood that lies across his path. A sinister place, it is made more foreboding in that its inhabitants are foul creatures whose energies are devoted to the destruction of those intent on reaching the castle on the hill. Until entering the wood, the

[1] *The Cathedral*, Macmillan, 1946, p. 295.

traveller is happy. But once in it, his confidence vanishes. Everything seems subtly changed. Weapons that once seemed powerful now are useless. All in which formerly he put his trust is without any force. Worst of all is the feeling that he himself is changed. He fears that he has become like the gibbering monsters surrounding him.

Tolstoy, at about the age of fifty, passed through the dark wood. He has told us how life lost its zest and everything seemed woefully altered. This happened in spite of the fact that nothing was visibly different. "All this," he declares, "took place at a time when so far as all my outward circumstances went, I ought to have been completely happy. I had a good wife who loved me and whom I loved; good children and a large property which was increasing with no pains taken on my part. I was more respected by my kinsfolk and acquaintances than I had ever been; I was loaded with praise by strangers; and without exaggeration I could believe my life already famous. Moreover I was not insane nor ill." Everything, however, had lost its savour. All on which he had built his life seemed to be a mockery. Tolstoy was fortunately rescued from this state of mind and his life re-created by a second birth. God broke into his life in such a way that it was re-shaped, re-modelled and given new impetus and meaning.

There are a number of men and women who, having driven themselves hard during youth and early adulthood, become uneasy at the stage marked by the forty, forty-five, fifty age-line. They have reached life's mid-point. In some of the reaches of the dark wood through which they are passing then, they come to feel acutely alone.

The renowned psychiatrist, Dr. Carl Jung, stresses the importance of this period normally too little emphasized. Jung believes that a different psychological approach is needed to deal with people at this time. In treating folk up to this stage, he says, the methods and principles of his colleagues, Freud and Adler, are adequate. But as life proceeds there is a marked change in the elements of the psyche and a new approach is needed. This is so important that we should distinguish between a "psychology of the morning" and a "psychology of the afternoon".

With women there are vital bodily changes occurring about this time. The need for readjustment of a mental and emotional character is, therefore, more readily understood and accepted by them. For many women this is a lonely and difficult stretch of the way. I have already suggested that many men go through an awkward stage as well. Some people say that this is because of physical changes too! What is really happening is that they have reached *middle-age*; and this term, and all it involves, is not acceptable to the person concerned. As C. G. Jung comments, the neurosis a man experiences at this time "comes mainly from his clinging to a youthful attitude which is now out of season". He is a youth no longer, and the waking up to the discovery is not palatable and is often resisted. When one is young, life stretches away into the limitless distance. Middle-age forcibly brings home the fact that, so far as *this* life is concerned, it is working towards a close—a close almost within sight. Dreams of achievement shrink to a size denying any consuming ambition.

All this need not be, and ought not to be. However, the fact is that for many this is an awkward time of adjustment. For them the "dark wood" symbolises harsh reality. Happy are they who emerge into the sunlight again!

It is worth noting that Bunyan's immortal story sets the mid-point in Christian's journey in the Delectable Mountains: a fitting description of where middle-age ought to find itself. The mistakes and follies of earlier life are over. One's powers are known and tested. The real worth and meaning of life should be understood and from the peaks of human endeavour one should be able to catch a glimpse of the Celestial City! Christian, in Bunyan's story, talks to four shepherds who reveal some facts about this important stretch of the highway. Among the unsuspected perils they disclose is a door in the side of the hill. Christian is told that it leads straight from where he stands to hell! The mid-stage of life's pilgrimage is evidently fraught with peculiar dangers.

\*　　\*　　\*　　\*　　\*

It is not as a religious commentator that C. G. Jung writes of these difficulties. His point of view is that of a psychologist. But in his book, *Modern Man in Search of a Soul*, there occurs this illuminating and oft-quoted sentence: "Among my patients in the second-half of life—that is to say, over thirty-five, there has not been one whose problem in the last resort was not that of finding a religious outlook on life. It is safe to say that every one of them fell ill because he had lost that which the living religions of every age have given to their followers, and none of them has been really healed who did not regain his religious outlook." [1]

In life's earlier stages it is possible to be shaken out of loneliness by some external event. A new interest can impel us into sharing it with others. Falling in love can do it; so can being won for some cause, or meeting a leader who sets emotions on fire. But after we have crested the brow of the hill our basic need is for something deeper. Without God, without a religious horizon, the landscape can look decidedly bleak whatever may be filling the foreground. At this stage we need a sense of His grip on us, and of the meaning and purpose created by that knowledge of His concern. Otherwise we can feel appalled at the frightening emptiness of what lies ahead.

A friend said to me, "In these last few years I have come to a new understanding of myself. When I was coming up the hill to the fifty mark I really had a wretched time. But I've got over it now—into a sort of second-wind. Actually,

[1] By kind permission of the publishers, Messrs. Routledge & Kegan Paul Ltd., we make these quotations from Dr. Jung's book.

I'm enjoying things now more than ever, and finding a thousand things to do—there's really not time for them all. It was a question of finding a new gear, realising that one was no longer going up the hill but at last coasting down it. Once you've made terms with that fact, everything's all right. It's all in God's way for us—that's what we've to discover."

It astonished me to realise that this friend had ever been in the kind of dilemma to which he referred. But it was so. At the mid-point he had been in peril of losing his way completely. He who had been so full of zest and energy withdrew into himself and looked like becoming a recluse and a misanthrope. Now, he is always the centre of a happy, laughing group of people. He works among boys, many of whom have found through him a way of inspiration. He finds time to write books, and appear on radio and television. The secret?—the discovery, at a deeper level, of the "loving, heart-rending secret of His way with us", and the acceptance of a new stage of life.

**9**

# The Best is Yet to Be

*To be old is a glorious thing when one has not unlearned
what it means to begin.*

MARTIN BUBER.

WHAT a benediction serene old age can pass on to the
rest of us! Today I spent an hour with a lady aged
ninety-eight. After visiting her and her eighty-year-old
daughter, I always feel a sense of elation and pride. One
has witnessed again the marvel of Christian old age
triumphing over all manner of difficulties.

Mrs. C. is blind. It is thirty-eight years since she lost her
beloved husband after a long illness during which she had
to be manager and part breadwinner as well as nurse. Two
years after his death her sight began to fail. In turn, her
daughter became her eyes, hands and feet. Because of this
daughter's loving kindness, theirs became increasingly a
fellowship of the heart.

To see the two of them together is to see real devotion.
To pray with them is to feel heaven near. To hear them
talk is to be struck with a deep sense of one's own ingrati-
tude. Without any mock piety—for pretence of any kind
is one of her aversions—blind Mrs. C. will say, "How thank-
ful we should be for all God's mercies! We should count
our blessings far more than we do."

What is it in this home that defeats loneliness and all
other perils to which others placed in similar circumstances
succumb so easily? The answer is simple. It is a sterling

Christian faith based on years of experience and forged in days of bitter trial. Said Mrs. C. to me this afternoon, "I know that He will see me through anything that happens."

Now that I come to write about loneliness and old age it is of the people who have defeated it that I think first of all. The spirit of Mrs. C. and her daughter is something I have seen equalled a number of times. There was an old man I used to visit in Gateshead with a handicap that kept him house-bound. This was very frustrating for he had been a vigorous man. The quality he showed in his late eighties was not so much serenity as an astonishing aliveness. His work had been that of a puddler, which, as anyone connected with the smelting industry knows, calls for a deal of stamina. Soon after I arrived in the north-east, he took me in hand, putting me through my paces in regard to the Tyneside dialect. "I'll see that you get to speaking like a native," he said. Every visit to him was a regular succession of "Why aye", "Why no", "Ha way hinnie", and so forth. Left on his own throughout the day, he was still undefeatable. He had the spirit of a lion.

The finest prayers I have ever heard in public—and by that I mean the prayers that seemed most real, urgent and beautiful—were uttered by an old lady who lived on her own in one room in inner London. In no circumstances could she be kept from the prayer-meeting at her chapel. There are many who remember Miss P. At the time few of us knew how old she was, nor how solitary her life, for we were all so busy about our own affairs! To think of her now is a benediction, and her prayers are still being answered —of that I am sure. In her presence one felt an inner stillness. She was "far ben" with God.

It is in old age that the quality of one's life is revealed. All superficial things are stripped away. Outer loneliness may come but if it meets with a lonely heart then the future of that person is sad indeed.

\*　　\*　　\*　　\*　　\*

In the previous chapter we considered the dangers of middle-age. It is interesting to compare two men and notice what changes can occur in the passing years. If ever you tread in the shadows of the "dark wood" it may help you to know that no less a person than John Wesley once passed through those shadows. The two men I want to compare are John Wesley at fifty-one with the same man at eighty-seven.

On Monday, 26th December, 1753, with the New Year just ahead, Wesley set down his customary entry in his *Journal*. That day he was feeling anything but well. He had made a disastrous marriage with Mrs. Vazeille, and for some months had been trying desperately to make something of it. His Quaker doctor had told him bluntly that he was so ill that he must not stay in town a day longer, adding, "If anything does thee good, it must be the country air, with rest, asses' milk, and riding daily." So, not being able to sit a horse, Wesley was taken by coach out to Lewisham, then in the country. In the evening, in order to prepare for the future and, as he put it, "to prevent vile panegyric", he wrote his epitaph! This he copied into his *Journal*. It is in this form:

*Here lieth*
*The body of John Wesley*
*A brand plucked out of the burning:*
*Who died of a consumption, in the fifty-first year of his age,*
*Not leaving, after his debts were paid, ten pounds behind him:*
*Praying,*
*God be merciful to me an unprofitable sinner!*

On January 1st, 1789, thirty-six years later, a veteran of eighty-seven greets the New Year with this entry in the same *Journal*: "If this is to be the last year of my life I hope it will be the best." What had happened? John Wesley, in spite of Molly Vazeille, the threat of consumption and the onset of middle-age, was not the man to stay long in the dark wood. God had grasped his life and was using him daily in evangelistic endeavour and in the building up of the churches. As life went forward, Wesley mellowed and matured. With "eye undimmed and natural strength unabated" he marched boldly forward into what is normally called old age, doing in an average day at least twice as much as a man half his years. The older he grew the more he was loved and venerated.

There is no need to report that the epitaph found on his tombstone is not the one composed in 1753, nor is what is there recorded set forth in that pseudo-apologetic vein. It is true to say that this man, under God, left for all time a shining example of what can be done in the second half of life. How do we account for this? First of all, and most of all, he was God's man, seeking to do God's business, and knowing God's reinforcement of health and power. For him there was no time for sitting idly by, or indulging in nostalgic reverie. He was daily challenged by human need and in touch with folk of all ages.

For him, as for all elderly people, there was a constant thinning of the ranks. All his earlier associates and helpers died before him. But, though this meant a deep sense of loss, it was a loss transfigured. Listen to his brother, Charles, writing of one of the company who had passed on. And remember that for them the mood of this hymn was not affectation but reality:

> *Rejoice, for a brother deceased,*
> *Our loss is his infinite gain;*
> *A soul out of prison released,*
> *And freed from its bodily chain;*
> *With songs let us follow his flight,*
> *And mount with his spirit above,*
> *Escaped to the mansions of light.*
> *And lodged in the Eden of love.*

I have a friend who once spoke to a very old man in Bristol whose grandfather remembered as a boy hearing

John Wesley preach. This was the recollection that was passed on across this bridge of the generations: "I remember seeing an old man with long white hair and a beautiful face; but the thing I remember most was not Wesley himself; it was the sight of tears coursing down the grimy cheeks of the Kingswood miners listening in their hundreds." This "old man with the beautiful face" was the King's messenger, always on the King's business. His was not a lonely heart, but one filled with compassion for his fellows. Those hard-bitten miners were moved as they heard him speak.

Who are those who most feel loneliness in old age? They are those whose state of mind is the reverse of that of a man like Wesley. They are acutely aware of the narrowing down of life, and of increasing bodily limitations. They have no link with the rising generation, are concerned with no good causes, and, indeed, are interested in nothing but their own welfare. Their love is not outgoing, but in-growing. Conscious of their ailments, they look back incessantly to the past as their peak period, the only time when they were really happy. They are conscious, too, of the fact that they survive temporarily in the midst of a dwindling company, having no hope of their survival, nor of their own when the inevitable time comes.

How right C. G. Jung was to point out that the fundamental need in the second half of life is that which only the living religions of the world can supply. This is needed now to make sense of life, and to open up the horizons that seem to be closing in, inevitably and grimly. All through life, the greatest discovery is God: or rather, to know that we are discovered by God: that He is interested in our individual lives and that we count with Him; and that we have a part to play in His plan that no one else can fill. We need to know now, more than ever, the realm of personal encounter with God: the world of *I and THOU* of which Martin Buber writes. That kind of knowledge is of utmost importance. Those who have it are, at this stage, still forward-looking and outgoing. As at every other stage, this is the first need to ward off loneliness in later life.

\* \* \* \* \*

E. S. P. Haynes, who wrote *The Lawyer's Notebooks,* was once looking at the journal of General Gordon. Gazing at one of the last entries, his eyes filled with tears. He was hardly able to read what was written. But it did not matter, for he knew what was there. Gordon, now understanding their full meaning, had copied out the lines of Charles Lamb:

> *I have had playmates, I have had companions*
> *In my days of childhood, in my joyful schooldays;*
> *All, all are gone, the old familiar faces.*

We know that mood, but it is not one to be indulged. Though our existing friends may not be able to talk of the old familiar faces, they are our *present* friends, and worth, therefore, a whole host of ghostly memories.

So the second rule for avoiding loneliness as the ranks begin to thin is to avoid overmuch nostalgia and backward glancing. The future is still what matters. The ship's company are all passing on. We shall meet again, in triumph!

\* \* \* \* \*

The third thing to note is that the wise person, consciously or unconsciously, does a great deal of preparation for this phase of life long before he enters it. Fairly early in life prudent people invest in insurance policies falling due about retiring age. How wise they would have been, at the same time, to develop an interest in worthwhile pursuits. This brings in a bountiful endowment later.

As life progresses we should steadily and definitely build a scale of values into our lives, safeguarding wise judgement and providing a sound basis for later years. *Those* are the things that will see us through our eventide, which thus can be either the fullest, or the emptiest period of our lives. These resources are needed and should be built into our very nature. They must be *within* us. At this period superficial things will not see us through.

"Remember thy Creator *in the days of thy youth*," counsels the writer of Ecclesiastes, "or ever the evil days come when thou shalt say I have no pleasure in them."[1] In order that all shall not be "vanity" or futility, we should get our bearings early. We can then heed Browning's invitation and prove it true:

> *Grow old along with me:*
> *The best is yet to be*
> *The last of life for which the first was made.*
> *Our times are in His hand*
> *Who saith, A whole I planned.*
> *Trust God, see all, nor be afraid.*

\*        \*        \*        \*        \*

There is a fourth rule. It is to learn to continue to fill our days with new and worthwhile enterprise. Pensions for officers in the old Indian Army were higher than those in the British Army—so a seventy-year-old retired soldier pointed out to Tom Hall,[2] the ex-Fleet Street editor. Retired Indian Army officers did not live as long: that was the

---

[1] It is thought that as this passage (Eccles. 12: 1–7) proceeds, the references are metaphors applying to the bodily life and functions in old age, e.g. "the house" is the body, and the "keepers" the hands, which often shake and tremble now. The "grinders" are the teeth! And it is the eyes through which one "looks out of the windows". "Or ever the silver cord (the spinal cord?) be loosed, or the golden bowl (the skull containing the brain?) be broken, or the pitcher (the heart) broken at the fountain, or the wheel (some other bodily function) broken at the cistern. Then shall the dust return to the earth as it was: and the spirit shall return unto God who gave it."

[2] This is mentioned in Tom Hall's book *Living Happily With a Heart*: a book which itself shows how it is possible to reorganise one's life, after sixty, and come to terms with heart trouble.

reason. On returning to settle down in this country their expectation of life upon retirement was not five years. Unable to reconcile themselves to their new conditions they died of sheer boredom.

It was George Bernard Shaw who said: "I want to be thoroughly used up when I die." John Wesley was of that type, too. In the latter's case, here was someone who lived for God and for his fellow-men, not afraid to look beyond the immediate horizon into the far distances. Wesley is reputed to have said, "I was never bored in my life." I can quite believe it. I can also imagine that he would have said, "I was never lonely either"—except, perhaps, for a twinge or two at fifty-one? Be not afraid!

## Part II

# Loneliness and Man

*"When you have shut your doors, and darkened your room remember never to say that you are alone, for you are not alone; but God is within and your genius is within."*

EPICTETUS

**10**

# Some Lonely People

> *In the deserts of the heart*
> *Let the healing fountain start.*
>                                 W. H. AUDEN

IT is possible at all stages of adult life to distinguish some
general patterns, or types of loneliness which continually
reappear. This chapter provides a fitting place where one
or two of these can be outlined and ways suggested by which
those so afflicted may escape.

Among the ranks of the lonely are some who have become isolated because of a complete lack of social graces.
Many of these people, in spite of a deep desire to be otherwise, are awkward and clumsy. A man once said to me, "I
feel myself to be a dead weight, a kind of non-conductor,
wherever I go."

If this, or anything like it, is true then let us begin by
acknowledging it. We start not by shrinking from facts.
Our very acceptance of them releases us from a certain
inhibition which in all likelihood will have been three parts
of our trouble.

Matters concerning rudeness, bad manners, lack of
thought for others concern habits which can be put right.
But we may have been trying to develop senseless social
graces to ingratiate ourselves with a set outside our social
orbit, or to join in pastimes for which we really have neither
taste nor ability. There is a revealing incident in the story
of Sisley Huddlestone, an outstanding American newspaper-

man. For years he mixed with the set that goes "huntin',
fishin', and shootin'". He was always desperately unhappy
in this milieu, for he had not the slightest interest or com-
petence in any of these sports. Suddenly in the midst of a
party where everyone was of this particular social set it
came to him that he did not need to behave as they did!
There was no force either within him or outside him
that compelled him to carry round a gun, or a fishing
rod. *He did not need to be doing these things at all.*
What a relief it was! He was immediately released from
an intolerable situation which for years had set him
apart.

After the initial acknowledgement of the fact, either that
we are not fashioned to be great social successes, or that
some social pastimes are unnecessary, we need to forget
what has been almost certainly the underlying cause of our
trouble—a fatal preoccupation with ourselves, and a stupid
desire to climb the social ladder. Instead, what is needed
is a concentration on *others*. And in our thought about
them we are no longer to consider them—as we have been
doing—as potential enemies and critics, but as friends.
When thrust among strangers we can start thinking: What
kind of folk are they? What motives animate them? What
are their real interests? How can I please them? When we
learn to ask such questions, we are finding the way out of
isolation.

Here is excellent advice for shy people. When entering
a room and feeling embarrassed, try looking ahead at someone, thinking: "Here is a fellow human-being, a would-be
friend of mine. I wonder whether he's happy? I'm going
to find out." All of us have the ability to touch other lives.
We have the initiative and need not wait for the other
person to contact us.

One of my friends once helped a shy, awkward fellow.
The latter felt he was a misfit, and that he lacked social
graces and the ability to make friends. Fortunately this

youth was amenable, accepting the suggestions that were made.

The treatment began with cross-examination: had he any interests? Yes, he liked photography. Then he should join a photographic club. He did: but not to enjoy it. No one took any notice of him, and he felt like a fish out of water. "All right," counselled my friend, "then start doing something helpful; make yourself generally useful. Think of yourself as a stranded fish trying to get back into the water."

Then he was told to go to a dance, but his verdict was that it was "terrible". "I can guess exactly what you did; as you came through the door, you glowered at everybody. Of course they reacted with: 'We'll have nothing to do with *that* chap!' But you must go again." The suggestions to shy people already outlined were passed on to him. At the next dance he was not a shining success, but it was not so "terrible". Eventually this youth became quite popular, and found a girl at the club to whom he is now happily married.

\* \* \* \* \*

Among the loneliest folk are the inordinately proud who have established barriers between themselves and others. An outstanding example of this type is Delius, the Bradford-born composer. His biography is a fascinating study—and a sharp warning. He became so fastidious that he was marooned in isolation. The blindness that overtook him was symbolic of the darkness in which he came to live. Without question, he was one whose pride and over-fastidiousness sent him into self-imposed isolation.

Do you know Edward Thomas's lines?

> *I built myself a house of glass,*
> *It took me years to make it,*
> *And I was proud. But now alas,*
> *Would God someone would break it.*

*But it looks too magnificent,*
*No neighbour casts a stone,*
*From where he dwells, in tenement,*
*Or palace of glass . . . alone.*[1]

Pride is an enemy of the most damaging kind. To take this enemy in, cosset him, and build up our life in his service is the height of folly.

Those who believe themselves superior are, in fact, inferior. We must not only associate with those whose society we automatically enjoy, but also with those who require an effort on our part. We need to develop strong, deep, and wide sympathies.

\*     \*     \*     \*     \*

Another facet of this complex problem is revealed by those who, whatever their age, are not fully mature. Their reactions to their fellows are still infantile. Joanna Field, the psychologist, made some interesting discoveries when, instead of studying other people, she began to observe herself and her own reactions. We can learn a great deal about ourselves, she says, from watching unhappy children. At one time she noticed that the motive really driving her was nothing more than: "I want to give a lot of people a lot of trouble!" Then she found herself making a fuss over a certain difficulty with the idea that if she showed enough distress someone would rush to help her; and then remembered that this, too, was a childish tactic. As a little girl when she had cried and said, "This is too difficult. I can't do it", someone had usually come to the rescue.

Next time you feel frustrated and miserable, watch yourself! Be careful that you do not give way to the childish

[1] Quoted with thanks to Messrs. Selwyn & Blount Ltd. (The Hutchinson Group).

desire to make everybody else suffer; do not succumb in the hope that someone will rush to help. Keep at it! You are living in an adult world.

One of the surest signs of maturity is the ability to enter into happy relationships with others. How many of us would have to admit that in our youth we were lamentably inadequate in this respect. We were locked up in the prison-house of self-consciousness.

Towards the end of the last century, there was a very personable young man at Oxford named Arthur W. Hopkinson. But if he seemed to be popular, confident and mature, he did not feel that way. He tells[1] how Winnington Ingram, later Bishop of London, made a deep impression upon him and many other undergraduates. At least once a year Ingram would come down to talk about the joys of life in Bethnal Green. Young Hopkinson was persuaded to join in the work of the settlement there. For him, he says, this was a time of liberation when he discovered what Liberty, Equality and Fraternity really meant. For the first time he was able to be natural and to find an outlet for a developing friendliness. He was far happier than he had ever been before. A year later, he became a theological student. The liberation process begun at Bethnal Green was continued and deepened. "I was," he says, writing very frankly about himself, "a late developer, but now I was beginning to find myself."

A number of us, in these matters, are "late developers", and some of us much later than Arthur Hopkinson. The half of life has gone, in some instances, before we find ourselves. This is a thought worth holding. It may be that our trouble is that of carrying adolescent attitudes into later years. If we are late developers, *now* is the time to speed the process of maturity.

Gaucherie, pride, childishness are all factors calculated to separate us from our fellows. They are typical states of

[1] In his book *Pastor's Progress*.

mind encouraging, or resulting in, isolation. Anyone so addicted must immediately take himself in hand. He needs to notice the specific points already outlined and to follow the advice offered in following chapters as we go deeper into the problem.

## II

# The Strangest Loneliness

*No wonder then so many die of grief,*
*So many are so lonely as they die.*
W. H. AUDEN

ONE summer's day just after the end of the war, I walked with crowds in holiday mood along the promenade at Skegness. Suddenly I caught sight of a man whose face and bearing revealed that he was totally out of tune with what was going on around him. His clothing was that issued to prisoners of war, a number of whom were still working on the land in that area. This young fellow looked like a Pole or a Ukrainian, a non-German in the German army. Now, thousands of miles away from home, he was spending the day at a British holiday resort. I have rarely seen a man looking more miserable. Here he was, surrounded by a crowd of holiday-making people: they were happy, but he was not. Their language was not his; nor their ways either. Indeed, it was obvious that he was completely out of sympathy with them, perhaps still actively hostile.

For me that grim, solitary figure in blue jeans amidst a throng of laughing, excited, gaily-dressed people typifies what I would call the strangest loneliness—the loneliness made all the worse when one is enveloped by people: the loneliness amid the crowd.

I think I sensed this man's isolation all the more acutely because that week, away from the crowd, I had had a unique experience of fellowship with another man just like him.

This P.O.W. had been detailed to work on the farm where I had been staying. He, too, seemed utterly lost and lonely. One day I made an attempt to cross the barriers separating us. I asked him where he came from. He told me. At first we did not get on very well. "Me no speak English very good," he said. I told him that he was managing remarkably well. Then he did something not dependent on language. From his pocket he produced a wallet, and, like any soldier the world over, this Ukrainian sergeant showed me the inevitable snapshots. This was his home. That was the farm, and there was the corner of the farmstead that had been destroyed by a Russian bomb. Three or four snaps were shown in turn; and then, with deep pride and a nervous catch in his voice, he searched for an English word of description as he showed his last photograph, "And that," he said, "is my darling."

In spite of the limited vocabulary with which we could converse, I know that something happened during our brief, but important contact, for he went back to work a little less lonely than before. Thereafter we always had a smile and a nod for each other.

The figure of the prisoner of war looking so abject amid the swirling holiday crowds on the sea-front stands as a reminder that the mere presence of other people does not answer the problem. If contiguity could help then we should never be lonely amid the crowd. It is an odd thing that loneliness is far more a disease of towns and cities than of the countryside. The presence of a mass of people accentuates the problem. The root of the trouble is that we are not rightly related to the people around, nor they to us. The bigger the crowd, the greater our lack of relationship.

That is why a certain kind of advice frequently given to lonely folk is fruitless and irritating. It is no use telling them to "Get among people". Without waiting for our advice, the victim of loneliness has usually tried that, without relief. Being thrown into a group with whom one has no sympathy has about as much effect in producing fellowship as lobbing one more coconut into a bagful would have in causing the flesh and milk inside the nuts to mix. First the hard outer shells must be broken; then there can be a coming together to some profit. I remember the description one writer used of the mêlée of people in a tube train during the rush hour. They provided, he said, a "burlesque of human unrelatedness". The coconuts in the bag could scarcely be closer together, but in terms of fellowship, these human being could scarcely be farther apart.

How many people coming from the country to the city have found this a grim experience!

*He came to the desert of London Town*
*Grey miles long*

sang James Thomson of William Blake. Of how many others might those words have been written! Our cities can be such impersonal places; and the people living in them as hard and metallic as the offices and factories in which they work. Because town folk are surrounded by people with whom it is impossible, and sometimes inadvisable, to enter into relationship, they develop a shell difficult for strangers to penetrate.

In 1902 the German poet Rainer Maria Rilke came to Paris to meet Rodin. Shortly afterwards he wrote a thinly-disguised autobiographical book entitled *Notebooks of Malte Laurids Brigge* which makes clear what were the reactions of this hyper-sensitive young man to the city on the Seine. It begins, "People come here, then, to live? I should rather have thought they came here to die." To him Paris was the City of Dreadful Night, the Waste Land. To his friend Lou Andreas-Salomé he says that his first feeling in the city was of "a great fearful astonishment. . . . How lonely I was among these people, and continually denied by all I encountered. The cabs drove clean through me. . . ." He writes of "the drab, desolate sham life of these hypertrophied cities". Urban civilization, the poet saw, does something in itself to the inner being of the people compelled to live under its baneful influence. This works out not only in the standardization and the effects of mass suggestion described in the American documentary, *The Lonely Crowd,* but in an inward, spiritual isolation.

Rilke and his reactions to Paris are mentioned in Prof. Bouman's *Revolution of the Lonely.* After commenting that Rilke had read "but a few lines of the mystery which typifies the fate of the massed town-dwellers", he continues, "The town reveals the paradox of modern culture in its clearest form. Its roofs cover man's fate as he is dragged along ever faster, suffering from an ever-growing feeling of loneliness. It is not the silence of the countryside, where God has made nature and spirit visible, but the urban compression of individuals that has given birth to the deep loneliness that obscures directional awareness."[1]

\*    \*    \*    \*    \*

But it is not only the countryman coming to the city who is subject to the onset of loneliness. Moving away from one's environment, whether it be town or country, can provoke it. In the 1950's I received and accepted an invitation to join the teaching staff of Cliff College in Derbyshire. From the first my wife had secret misgivings. We lived in a beautiful house, with a wonderful view before us and the cliffs of Baslow Edge towering behind. Down in the valley flowed the Derwent. The village was a mile away, the nearest country town five miles, with Chesterfield and Sheffield over ten miles distant. The summers were glorious, but the winters long and hard. I

[1] *Revolution of the Lonely* (McGraw Hill), p. 51. Quoted by kind permission.

had my tutorial work, which was interesting and satisfying. My week-ends took me away on preaching engagements. But, as a number of my predecessors had discovered, the real stress of this appointment fell on wife and family. If they loved country life and were used to it, all was well. But for my wife, used to cities and to the busyness of church life, those years spent in the Peak District were, I am sure, the loneliest she has known. Never again, for her, the experiment of living in the remote country.

There was a time in the career of O. Henry, the great American short-story writer, when he was persuaded to attempt a rural life. His friends told him his work would improve if he could get away from New York and live amid the green fields.

Within a short time he was back again. "The country," he exclaimed, "I couldn't stand it. It drove me to distraction. The noise," he said—and he was speaking of the usual country sounds of birds, animals and so on—"was driving me mad. It prevented me from even thinking of work. I had to come back here for peace and quiet."

*Keep your splendid silent sun,*
*Keep your woods, O Nature, and the quiet places by*
*  the woods,*
*Keep your fields of clover and timothy, and your*
*  cornfields and orchards. . . .*
*Give me faces and streets—*
*. . . Give me the shores and wharves heavy-fringed with*
*  black ships!*
*O such for me! O an intense life, full to repletion and*
*  varied! . . .*
*People, endless, streaming, with strong voices, passions,*
*  pageants.*[1]

There speaks the incorrigible townsman who will be desperately lonely if he stays too long in the country.

[1] Walt Whitman: *Give Me the Splendid Silent Sun.*

There are, of course, dozens of cases of city folk finding their souls amid the quiet and peace and in the saner tempo of country living. The classic instance is that of Henry Thoreau, who left Concord and built a log-hut for himself by the side of Walden Pond, where he lived simply and in solitude. Paul Bloomfield, in his *Journal: 1939–49,* tells of a time when he was reading Thoreau's *Walden* in a train. Two American G.I.'s in his compartment had never heard of the book. They could not believe that Thoreau had voluntarily chosen solitude. "Was there a girl in it?" asked one of them. When told that there was not, he added, "I guess he must 'a been crazy!"

\* \* \* \* \*

Norman MacLean, Moderator of the Church of Scotland in 1927, was born and bred in the Gaelic-speaking Isle of Skye. He was used to the hills, the sea and the shore in that magnificent, if, to some of us, rather lonely, setting. At the age of thirteen he was offered the chance of education at an academy in far-away Inverness. In the second book of his autobiography, *Set Free,*[1] he gives a picture of his impressions on arrival in the city. He was amazed at the number of people about him—amazed and almost terrified. He knew no one except his elder brother, and when, after a day or so, John had to leave to go on to St. Andrew's University, young Norman felt utterly alone.

Two remarkable experiences came to him within a day or two of each other. On the Saturday after his brother left him, he walked by the river Ness and sat on a seat, going over his problems, feeling the most solitary soul in all Scotland. So miserable was he, he says, that he found himself questioning the worthwhileness of existence, and whether it had any meaning or purpose. A breeze was blowing up from the west, working against the tide, bring-

[1] Published by Hodder & Stoughton of London, to whom acknowledgement is made.

ing the salt water from the ocean, and the spume was rising from the river. Then—it happened: radiant, from behind a cloud, the westering sun poured a flood of light upon everything. It was touched to unbelievable beauty. The drops of water were iridescent, the whole scene glorious.

"I do not know what many-syllabled name the modern psychologists give to that experience," writes the Moderator. "I had it only twice in my life, though I have longed to have it again. For the joy of it, if but momentary, was the most exquisite in life. It was as if a veil was withdrawn in a great temple and the eyes saw for a moment the inner-most shrine where the god dwelt in isolated glory. For a fleeting moment the Creative Life at the core of the Universe broke visibly through the material crust that veils it."

The next day, still alone, Norman went to the High Church where he was given something he had never seen before—a hymn book. Those were austere days for religion in Scotland. The islanders back in Skye denounced the practice of singing hymns in church. I suppose they thought, in some way, it was idolatrous. In other places in Scotland, hymns were only just coming into favour. In the service in which this boy shared, the metrical psalms and paraphrases were used in the first part; the hymn, on that memorable night, came at the end. As the voices surged in a burst of singing the like of which he had never known, there came the verse:

> *But what to those who find? Ah! this*
> *Nor tongue nor pen can show;*
> *The love of Jesus, what it is*
> *None but His loved ones know.*

An old lady, near by, was unashamedly weeping into her handkerchief—and the boy from Skye suddenly found himself right in the midst of the experience which the hymn was declaring "None but His loved ones know".

Two things had spoken to this "little, freckled, red-haired boy in the back pew of the deep gallery" who "sat down shaken and trembling". The day before, the river Ness had been the vehicle by which God had spoken to him in the beauty of nature. Now the Lord Jesus had knocked on this boy's heart and been let in. The loneliness was over for good—in Inverness and anywhere.

Let Norman MacLean finish his own story: "At last the old lady rose to go, and turned to me as if she noticed me for the first time. She smiled and stretched out her hand to me. As I look back, that handshake was a sacrament, linking age and youth in the love of God. I walked to my lodging through a new-made world." He was lonely no more!

To those who, in any form, experience what I have called "the strangest loneliness" the challenge is to find a new and better relation with other people. How to achieve this is the theme to which we turn in later chapters.

**12**

# Our Place of Work

*Where the many toil together,*
*There am I within my own.*
      HENRY VAN DYKE

THREE pictures vividly etched in my memory set the
scene for this chapter. The first concerns a day in war-
time when I was shown round a canning factory. The girls
in one section were preparing food for the troops in
Burma. The mixture included fish, egg and curry. It
was an unpleasant-looking as well as a somewhat evil-
smelling concoction. Upstairs I found another group
packing golden puddings. "What a difference!" I exclaimed involuntarily to the personnel manager accom-
panying me. We had come all the way from the sour to
the sweet, and I felt it in the atmosphere. "Do you know,"
replied my companion, "I don't have a tenth of the trouble
with the girls in this department that I have in the other.
And still the management won't realise that there's more
to this business than just paying out wages at the end of
the week!"

There is indeed far more to this matter of relationship
to work than the consideration merely of monetary
reward. Modern social psychologists have astonished the
materialistically-minded in the management-and-employer
group by producing facts and figures underlining the point
made by the personnel manager of that canning factory!
What we work amongst affects our mentality and our out-

look. The conditions in which work is done are far more important than previous generations have assumed.

As a probationary minister I lived in an area east of London. Thousands of people in that district found employment at a huge factory at Dagenham, and most of them were happily settled. Mr. C., two doors from where I lived, quite enjoyed the conditions of work, but not Mr. D., my landlady's husband. He loathed every minute of it and said so. To him there was something soul destroying about the mass-production methods. He did not like the way commissionaires stood and watched the men in and out. They were not above "frisking" them at times to see that they were not carrying anything away.

Mr. D. had been a fitter in the Clyde shipyards. Those were the years of mass unemployment, and he had left Glasgow for the only work that offered—in the mammoth car factory. Some years later he left Dagenham because he could endure it no longer, returning to his real work as a skilled craftsman among his own folk on the Clyde. When I met him again I scarcely recognized him. Now he had pride and independence. There was a glint in his eye and a lilt in his voice. Before, though he brought home good wages, he was an unhappy man without spirit.

The third picture is of an adolescent, keen, eager. He had enjoyed his last years at school. He had many friends, and was popular with everyone. Beneath a mop of fair hair, shining blue eyes looked straight at you: an attractive boy. Then he went to work. The gleam left his eyes, and the freshness vanished from his appearance. His experiences at work took from him not only his confidence but his whole zest for living. What went wrong? The chief thing was that no one took any notice of him. He was allowed to drift into his job in the yard without anyone seeming to care or take the slightest interest. There was no one there of his own age. And the older men, whose habits and conversation disgusted him, ignored him altogether.

They gave him guidance about his work only when the foreman complained. Here was a depressed and despondent youth, all the more tragic because he had promised so well.

Our place of work, whether it be office, university, mine, house, shop or factory is a determining factor of greatest importance. It is not only that we spend most of our time there, but it is also the place where we gain a sense of status. It is our work that helps very largely to give life its meaning.

J. A. C. Brown stresses these facts in his book *The Social Psychology of Industry*. He endorses what I have said in a previous chapter concerning our basic need for love and emotional security. He traces this back to the biological situation when we come into the world as helpless infants depending on others for food, shelter and everything connected with well-being.

Implanted in us, then, is a deep need for love and emotional security. In adult life, says J. A. C. Brown, this takes the form of a desire for status and function in society. We need to know three things: (1) that we count as an individual, (2) that other people are interested in us and recognize our contribution to the scheme of things, and (3) that at some point we form part of a team. That is why loneliness at work is much more serious than is sometimes realised. We are denied true status and function. Our colleagues are not recognizing us. We have no place in what is going forward. We do not belong to the team. It is for these reasons that unemployment is much more than a condition of "idleness from work with the state providing subsistence money". Unemployment takes away our dignity as workers, denies us any function, and cuts us off from the community of working people.

"Loss of status," says J. A. C. Brown,[1] "leads to social

[1] These references from *The Social Psychology of Industry* are by permission of the publishers, Penguin Books Ltd.

isolation and is one of the commonest causes of neurosis."
For some years I worked on Tyneside, an area hard hit by
pre-war depression. When I was there, after the outbreak
of war, everybody able to work was back in employment.
But it was still a depressed area. It felt like a district
that had taken a beating, and it was a long time before
it recovered. The people were dispirited, and this through
no fault of their own. Behind everything was the fear of
redundancy returning. By living amongst those gallant
people I came to understand a little of what unemployment can do to people's souls.

*    *    *    *    *

In certain forms of occupation, loneliness is fostered by
actual conditions of solitude. I knew a young man who was
posted during the war to an isolated radar station on the
rugged coast of Ireland. He spent days at a time with no
company but his own. Before that experience he was a
lively fellow. He emerged a neurotic problem.

Lighthouse-keepers are never allowed to do duty alone.
Two men, at least, man a station. A little while ago many
people must have been intrigued by a B.B.C. announcement
that because of a quarrel with his companion, a lighthouse-
keeper was to be relieved. As soon as one thought about
this one could see why. The danger would be not so much
from inflamed tempers as from the risk of psychological
damage caused by the isolation resulting from the quarrel.
In those lonely conditions, two men not speaking to one
another would be two men in real jeopardy.

Some of us know what it is to be separated from our
fellows even whilst surrounded by them. We have all heard
of men being "sent to Coventry". Racial prejudice can also
encourage this cruel situation. The one odd-man-out in
any group is always in danger of isolation. By adopting
methods of cold-shouldering, heartless men can cause much
harm.

In 1959 there was a strike at the works which we have already mentioned at Dagenham. It has been estimated that as a result something like six million pounds were lost in production and wages. In the car-door section of the works a welder had ceased to pay his union dues. The others retaliated by refusing to work with a non-union man. In the end, the strikers went back with this man still on the pay-roll. "I don't intend to join a union, or get another job," he is reported to have said. "I shall be at work on Monday. It will be difficult to work alongside men who hate the sight of me, but I don't care what they think." It was a brave statement, and for two or three days after the resumption of work he stood by what he had said. But the inevitable pressure told in the end. His wife finally urged him to leave and find employment elsewhere.

I have known other men similarly ostracized by their fellows because of some Trade Union issue, and have discovered how desperate their position can become. Two men, members of rival railwaymen's unions, lived next door to one another and were firm friends at home and at work. Their wives, too, were very friendly. Then came a strike supported by one union and not by the other. One man, therefore, since he continued working, was a blackleg. An intolerable situation arose between these two men and their households, once so closely knit together. The black-leg had to face great hostility from his old friend as well as from his workmates.

This situation is made no easier when found in other places—in school or, more importantly, the home. Ostracism, for whatever reason, is evil and should be instantly tackled wherever it is found.

\* \* \* \* \*

What advice is to be offered to the person suffering loneliness at work? First, he would be wise to take stock of himself, his occupation and its conditions. He may be shocked to discover that he is his own worst enemy. He may be holding to some human habit hurtful to himself and offensive to others. He should be ready, for the sake of those dear to him, to change his ways. There are a number of small irritating habits which are often the spark for domestic and business conflagrations. You do not wear a sports jacket at a wedding. Only after drastic surgery do square pegs fit into round holes.

After several years in the teaching profession, a brilliant graduate whom I knew recognised that boys would not accept him and that teaching staffs found him incompatible. A forthright colleague told him he was in the wrong occupation. He took the advice and is now doing research work. The result is that he is happy in his work with colleagues who readily accept him.

We should not make ourselves martyrs to intolerable and unsuitable conditions. In other words, a great deal of loneliness is unnecessary and of our own making. We blame other people and our conditions for a state which, in reality, is often our personal responsibility.

A special form of work-time separation and ostracism is endured by some sincere Christians. There are certain everyday situations in which religious convictions divide one immediately from the crowd. A Christian girl I knew worked at a skilled profession which, for some unaccountable reason, has always attracted girls of light morals. In her particular case it needed a great struggle to maintain her standard. Two other girls I knew were employed in the head office of a large insurance concern. Annually at Christmas something of a drinking orgy was staged at the close of business. Both these girls had strong Christian convictions about moral behaviour and refused alcoholic drink. But so persistent were their so-called friends that champagne was literally forced down the throat of one of them. For a time both had to face ridicule and ostracism.

However, by sheer strength of Christian principles these girls finally won through. Christianity is not a matter of taboos and restrictions, but of positive living. These girls refused to be deflected or defeated. They also refused to lose their tempers and, equally, to lose their sense of humour. Those office drinking parties are now a thing of the past. No juniors are forced to share in something to which they conscientiously object. Who, and what, has won the victory?

The ostracized member of any community must not only have courage but must take up a *positive* attitude to what is happening. A negative approach only results in loneliness and failure. We must try to understand others and comprehend what is the cause of their behaviour. To understand is often to pardon.

The sad fact is that Christians, witnessing for their Lord, are sometimes in danger not of helping, but hindering His cause. They are wise to listen to what He has to say. They must learn to be in the world and yet not of it. Our Lord, as always, is Himself our example. He never lowered His standard, yet He was "the friend of publicans and sinners". He found a way to show friendship and compassion to all manner of people and to leap across all barriers. Being a witness does not mean being difficult. It means the opposite; it means being like Him.

There will be times when we shall have to clench our teeth and bear ridicule and opposition. Our Lord tells us this. To His first disciples He said, "In the world you shall have tribulation" (which, whatever else it implies, means testing), "but be of good cheer, for I have overcome the world". "Blessed are ye," He told His disciples, "when men shall persecute you and say all manner of evil against you falsely, for my sake. Rejoice and be exceeding glad, for so persecuted they the prophets which were before you."

We must determine to behave in such a way as to win victories, not suffer defeats. God can take a difficult situation and use it. One of the reasons why in so many places Christianity is not winning its battles is because so few people are fighting effectively.

What we need to remember is this: as surely as in our place of worship we must practise His Presence in our place of work. The opportunity is ours.

## 13

# In Times of Temptation

*What's done we partly may compute*
*But know not what's resisted.*
ROBERT BURNS

THERE is an aspect of loneliness that finds expression in people suffering from the stress of wrong impulses. They often imagine their temptations to be unique. "Other people," they say to themselves, "know nothing of this. They live on a different level." So they judge. To them it seems impossible that anyone else can experience these destroying forces. For that reason they feel cut off from their fellows.

This condition needs to be regarded seriously. It has proved to be a dominant factor in a number of suicide attempts, mainly among students. Faced with overwhelming temptation, feeling dejected and isolated, many people have added the burden of a sense of guilt to their overwrought condition by not distinguishing between temptation and actual sin. They feel themselves to be pariahs, social misfits. Whatever other people's opinion may be, these poor folk feel separated and even doomed.

In general this is an adolescent problem, more often than not associated with the new faculties and emotions connected with sex. But the experience is by no means confined to youth, nor to this one aspect. Many face this kind of problem in later years. We have spoken of the testing time of middle-age and the symbolism of the "dark wood". The problem of being fifty, one of my friends confessed, proved to be one of the most difficult he has had to handle. He found himself beset by all manner of insidious temptations, including that of distrusting life itself. It was difficult at the same time as he felt this sense of life's emptiness to bear the sarcastic jibes of the young, themselves irritatingly unaware of the problem. Because none of his associates had ever warned him, nor had they seemed conscious of such a stage, my friend believed he was alone in his melancholy. So for him, too, there was added to all these difficulties a sense of isolation.

One way of deliverance is to find someone with whom to discuss the secret and private fear. It is to be noted that, though equally difficult, these temptation problems do not usually cause so much anguish at fifty as they do at fifteen precisely because of the increasing wisdom and balance of maturity. In later life we are more inclined to take some positive action. My friend, for instance, went to see his doctor who soon enlightened him, and suggested that he should talk frankly about his troubles to one or two contemporaries. This he did, and was amazed to discover that his experiences were not unique. That discovery helped him greatly.

My advice to anyone enduring the mental isolation of temptation is to seek out a trusted friend with whom it can be discussed. Any problem of this character needs to be brought into the light of day.

In a very frank way, Victor Gollancz, the publisher, has discussed the troubles that beset him as a youth.[1] He found himself enduring the deepest sense of isolation, weighed down by an intolerable sense of guilt. It had to be exorcised, he says, by that "co-operation between the human and the divine of which the words Jesus Christ are the final expression" (the reference is to the phrase at the end of Romans 7 where, after asking "Who shall deliver

[1] In his book *My Dear Timothy*, quoted by kind permission.

me?", Paul cries, "I thank God, through Jesus Christ our Lord").

Gollancz had to learn that there is a sane and satisfactory expression for the sex instinct. The chapter in which he discusses this is rather dramatically entitled "Hell". His experiences fully justified that title, however, for at the age of sixteen he was told by another youth, who accused him, that for his abuses there was no deliverance and no forgiveness, and that certain physical results were inevitable. All this the boy, already labouring under a burden of guilt, accepted without question. The world lost its radiance, and for three or four months, writes Gollancz, he lived in the pit of despair. Then, by the grace of God, he made a resolution—to consult the family doctor, a down-to-earth Scotsman who set matters aright. Life was good again.

What damage can be done by false notions secretly carried! A frank discussion with a mature and understanding counsellor is the answer. There is no need to endure Hell!

In some cases we, too, might consult the family doctor, or see a psychiatrist. Ensure, however, that the specialist is a practising Christian. The minister is there for just such an hour as this, for it is only in God that complete freedom and forgiveness can be found.

I remember years ago listening to that engaging writer and broadcaster S. P. B. Mais, discussing his radio experiences when talking to children. Mais spoke so understandingly to youngsters that they warmed to him immediately. He told us of a broadcast that had a strange sequel. From all over the country young people had written to him, making him their confidant. It was because to them he was just a friendly voice that they confided things which they would never have dreamt of telling their own family or friends.

Without doubt it is the impersonal aspect of the

confessional that helps those who use it. Shy people should remember that they can go to another church for this almost forgotten spiritual therapy. It is an act meant to be impersonal. The absolution pronounced is God's. The human voice is but a channel. The forgiveness comes only from the Father.

Here we are well advised to pause. Protestants are rightly suspicious of the mechanical application of this principle, and dislike anything resembling priestcraft. But I am convinced that when Christ gave men the power to forgive sins, He passed on something real and of utmost value. I am equally sure that this power was not meant to be canalised or mechanically applied. There is behind John 20:21 ff. no authority for special *priestly* absolution. In this sense, and for this purpose, all the Lord's people are priests. I shall never forget an occasion when I came face-to-face with someone tortured by a fearful sense of guilt. The ordinary references to God's forgiveness would not do. I had to assert, absolutely, dogmatically and definitely that this child of God *was* forgiven. I knew that it was so, and I knew I had to say so *in the power of the Holy Spirit*.

So for sin there is confession and forgiveness. For temptation there is admission and discussion. And with this frank sharing comes the realisation that we are not alone in our testing experience. Temptation and sin are known to every human being. "If we say that we have no sin," says John, "we deceive ourselves and the truth is not in us . . ." Paul in 1 Corinthians 10: 13 comments, "There hath no temptation taken you but such as is common to man." Dr. Weymouth's translation is even more forceful: "No temptation has you in its power but such as is common to human nature."

The verse continues in words supremely helpful: "But God is faithful, who will not suffer you to be tempted above what ye are able: but will with the temptation also make a way to escape, that ye may be able to bear it."

When we go deeply into the matter we discover that in times of temptation *we can have fellowship with God*. It is the experience of being put to the test, and re-discovering our need of Him, that drives us closer to Him. We find Him, thus, a present help in our time of trial.

\* \* \* \* \*

In regard to temptation we need to understand clearly that it means "being put to the test". Temptation is not sin even though it may be its prelude. Our Lord Himself knew temptation. Of course we are not alone in it. The best, and the worst, know its onset though circumstances may differ. We need never think that these disturbing thoughts make us less than men. The fact that we are tempted proves we *are* men. Carlyle, in *Sartor Resartus*, proclaims: "Name it as you choose: with or without visible Devil, whether in the natural Desert of rocks and sands, or in the populous Desert of selfishness and baseness—to such Temptation are we all called. Unhappy if we are not! Unhappy if we are but Half-men, in whom that divine handwriting has never blazed forth. . . ."

Rabbi Joshua Liebman, author of *Peace of Mind*, thinks that the first of the commandments of the new morality we should engrave upon our heart is "Thou shalt not be afraid of thy hidden impulses". Our Lord was not! He admitted to the unworthy thoughts that came to Him—for only through His sharing could the disciples have come to know of the Temptations. Says Dr. A. E. Day, "It could not have been easy for one who lived on so high a plane and had such a momentous sense of mission to confess that it ever occurred to him to try to turn stones into bread or to make a spectacular, crowd-arresting leap from the pinnacle of the Temple or to bow down to Satan. But Jesus admitted it all to his friends, and of course to himself." Here is our Lord Himself acting according to this deep psychological wisdom. We are not to be shocked by thoughts that come, nor by unworthy desires that rise within our minds. We are to be honest and admit their existence to ourselves and, if necessary, be prepared to confess them to others. What matters is, however, what we do with them. The dark vanishes when we let the daylight in.

Our Lord faced His testings in the certainty of the Father's companionship and guidance. He answered all suggestions to take an easier path by reference to God's way. It was, indeed, because other ways offered that He knew more certainly what God's ways were. His method of defeating temptation should be ours—looking to God and claiming His Presence and His Promises.

Thus temptation, instead of being a lonely experience, becomes something reminding us of our fellowship with Jesus, bringing us into closer communion with Him. The victory that He ensures is the goal and purpose behind all our testing—development into the likeness of Christ Jesus our Lord.

## 14

# When Bereavement Comes

*They are all gone into the world of light!*
*And I alone sit lingering here;*
*Their very memory is fair and bright,*
*And my sad thoughts doth clear.*
                              HENRY VAUGHAN

A FRIEND was telling me what happened to him a
fortnight after the death of his father. "We thought
we were getting on fairly well," he said. "Dad's death had,
of course, been a terrible blow. But we had been prepared
for it. And we faced it as Christians. The family and
friends came and went. From all over the world poured
in messages of sympathy—and then it happened. Suddenly, one afternoon, I realised that I faced the point of
no return. This was *it*. Never more now would I hear
father's voice, nor discuss business with him. This was the
end."

The experience so flooded him with anguish that, he
says, he had never known anything like it. Now, my friend
is one who, in the war days, had to take part in each of
the allied invasions in turn, and since then has had to
face difficult times. Often he has known what it is to be
alone, and make decisions on his own initiative. But what
happened a fortnight after his father's death was different.
He was struck by a piercing sense of loneliness; and this,
though he enjoyed his work, was happily married, and had
numerous friends.

Many have experienced a similar loss and felt somewhat similar emotions—realising that this is "the point of no return". The situation is one which, in some form, all must face. We cannot avoid it. And when it comes it is as if something of ourselves had gone. Life, we feel, can never be the same again. In that, of course, we are right. But life *can* be renewed and rebuilt in a new way without morbidity or loneliness.

The most acute test comes for most of us when the flurry is over, the funeral past, and sympathetic friends gone. *Then* we know what it is to be alone. We come to times that before were occasions of sharing; and now there is no one. Instead we face the emptiest moments possibly we shall ever know.

A working man told me that shortly after his wife's death he was given a substantial rise in salary. Coming home that night to an empty house was terrible. "*She* would have been so pleased," he said, "and now she was not there." Says Dr. Leslie Church, in his little book *Yonder,* about similar desolating experiences: "We must sit alone and see an empty chair, or trudge without the dear companion by our side. We shall miss the one we see no more. Our hearts will cry out in terrible longing." But Dr. Church goes on to point out that if our faith be in God we shall learn not to mourn for our loved ones. The Eternal God will not betray our trust. We shall discover how to take up again the tasks of daily living.

I can hear someone in the pit of this dark experience asking "But how can these things be?" Relief seems so far away. There are certain considerations that should be thought over in answer: the first of a preliminary character, the second more final. Let us look at them.

\* \* \* \* \*

The first thing I would say is that it is wise to let grief have its outlet. Our Lord wept. There is nothing wrong with tears. God has provided a way of expressing emotions and finding a way of physical relief. There is no value at such a time in the stiff-upper-lip philosophy. The idea that to give way to grief is unmanly has done great harm. What one needs to do is to pray, and to pour out one's inner feelings to God. To bring our private affairs before Him is not an intrusion. It is what He wants. The Father is more than able to comfort His child if the child will but seek Him.

"Steady down"—that is a further piece of advice some people need. We are not to rush about in a state of emotional instability, nor to make sudden and wild decisions about our future: selling the house, or cashing securities. A friend who has counselled many at these difficult times makes it an axiom that no drastic change should take place for at least six months. We must formulate our decisions calmly and wisely, and seek the guidance of God in our affairs. Whatever we do, just because we feel alone, we must not rush to fill the gap.

Another point to be noticed is that though grief should be allowed expression, the one thing to be shunned is self-pity. That is morbid. Grief is not. There is a positive and definite answer to the person who asks, "What have I to live for now?" The answer is bigger than the small matter of our personal grief. We must find fulfilment in work, and in service for others. Sometimes it is possible to do something in continuation of the loved one's special interests. Here is a real fulfilment. It is possible, too, through our own experience, to discover that we are in a unique position to help others. Paul speaks of the "God of all comfort" in 2 Corinthians 1:3, and continues "who comforteth us in all our tribulation, that we may be able to comfort them which are in any trouble, by the comfort wherewith we ourselves are comforted of God." The love which now we cannot share must not be allowed to wither —it can be passed on to others needing our help.

Feelings of remorse or recrimination are not to be indulged. All of us are tempted to stab ourselves with sharp
remembrances of unkind acts and missed opportunities.
What shall we do when these negative thoughts come upon
us—perhaps with good reason? Take them to God! His
forgiveness is a reality, and it is there for just such a
time as this. We must let our past mistakes make us more
understanding towards those who are with us now.

Life does not stand still. We must go forward. I have
known folk who have kept their loved one's room, or the
house, "just as it was"—like the wedding table at Miss
Havisham's. Clothes or other articles are cherished like
fetishes or idols. Among the many useful things which
Dr. J. S. Bonnell has to say about grief in his book, *No
Escape from Life*[1], is the story of how that very level-
headed person, Madame Curie, fell into this trap. After her
husband Pierre had been killed in a street accident she
kept his blood-stained clothes. She would take them out
and kiss them—until finally her sister took them out and
burned them. The way for us, and the way our loved
one would have us find, *is forward.*

We must also guard against seclusiveness. We should
endeavour to mix naturally with other people and make
a point of continuing habits of worship. The first visit to
church *alone* can be a disturbing experience. But the very
taking of this step will help us to realise that we are not
alone. "A recluse," someone once said, "is not a hero."
We must not run away, nor adopt a grim defeatist attitude.
We need to show courage, as well as faith, hope and love.

\*    \*    \*    \*    \*

In facing what are the still deeper considerations about
this matter it is well to start with the realisation that life
on earth is inevitably a life of partings—and of final part-

[1] Published by Arthur James, Ltd., Evesham, Worcs.

ings, too. Francis Thompson, writing of Daisy, tells how she went "her unremembering way":

> She went and left in me
> The pang of all the partings gone,
> And partings yet to be.

Those pangs come to us all, for they are part of the material of life on this earth. In his book significantly entitled *Near the Brink*, Dr. L. P. Jacks confesses that the event that had shaken him most during the previous ten years was the loss of his wife, with whom he had shared fifty-six years in marriage. Her death, he says, forced upon him a truth which "even a nonagenarian is capable of forgetting"— that life in all its forms is "death-ended". "Until we have realized that death is integral to life," he writes, "the price we pay for life, and for love, the highest manifestation of life, we know little about ourselves, and as little or less about our neighbours."[1]

This, then, is a fact with which we must come to terms without morbidity. Partings are inevitable. They leave us, however, with two things: our memories, and the knowledge of how richly blessed we have been in love and companionship.

We are "strangers and pilgrims". The writer of the Letter to the Hebrews, who would have us recognize this, takes glory in it. In Chapter 11 he writes of the heroes of faith who lived their lives in the full understanding of life's greater background, accepting their destiny as strangers and pilgrims. Their roots were not in this earth, for they sought the city that hath foundations, whose builder and maker is God.

> Life is probation and the earth no goal
> But the starting-point of man

[1] Quoted by kind permission of the publishers, Messrs George Allen & Unwin Ltd.

writes Robert Browning. Ours is a greater destiny than can be fulfilled here.

Above all others we are wise to listen intently to what Jesus has to say. In the Upper Room He talked to His disciples on the night when He was to be betrayed, the day before He was to die and be parted from them. "In my Father's house are many abiding places; if it were not so, I would have told you; for I go to prepare a place for you . . . I come again, and will receive you unto myself; that where I am, there ye may be also." In those words is all we need to know: they imply our personal immortality in a substantial spiritual environment. Though all the conditions will be changed—it being a spiritual life—there will be for us what we think of as "a place". It will fit us and suit us, for it has been prepared by Him. He comes for His own! And fellowship is continued there—fellowship with Him, and therefore, we are assured, with our loved ones too.

\*     \*     \*     \*     \*

When my mother died it was a crushing blow. It was unexpected not because the doctors had not warned us, but because I could not accept it. As I have described elsewhere, I was praying for a miracle to happen. Then God Himself changed the form of my prayers. I knew the miracle was not to be. On her last night I prayed that she might be allowed to slip away quietly into the life beyond. She did so, and the last words of which she was conscious were those of the 23rd Psalm . . . "Yea, though I walk through the valley of the shadow of death, I will fear no evil: for Thou art with me. . . ."

As the months went by I experienced a wonderful thing. It came without my seeking, but it was real and not in the least morbid. At times of private prayer I became aware not only of communion with God but also with my mother. I felt a certainty of her well-being and safety. Just that, and nothing more. But it meant a great deal to me. After a while the experience vanished but there have since been times when it returned : when I have been engaged on some important task, or when I have had to make a decision of particular significance. These occasions have been real but, again I repeat, not in the least morbid. These experiences were quite the reverse.

The fact, as all bereaved Christians should come to know, is that our departed ones have a share in the background of our lives. I do not mean that we rest in the memory of an erstwhile relationship, but that we have a continued sense of companionship.

I quoted from the Letter to the Hebrews. We should look at that magnificent paragraph in Chapter 12 in which the writer contrasts the old dispensation, under Moses, with the new, under Christ. He recalls the picture of the highest manifestation known in Old Testament days—the semi-material manifestation of God at Mount Sinai, with its cloud, thick darkness, earthquake, fire and terrifying voice. Then, in contrast, he describes the communion open to Christians when we come to worship. "But ye are come unto mount Sion, and unto the city of the living God, the heavenly Jerusalem, and to innumerable hosts of angels, to the general assembly and church of the firstborn, which are written in heaven, and to God the Judge of all, and to the spirits of just men made perfect, and to Jesus the mediator of the new covenant. . . ." We are compassed about by a great cloud of witnesses.

Let us not forget that vision of the heavenly company. When we gather together to find fellowship with God they are associated with us.

On December 3rd, 1663, Richard Baxter wrote some verses headed with the words: "Written when I was silenced and cast out." These verses serve to remind us of sources of remedy for our loneliness which are too little regarded; and of possibilities of communion into which too few of us have entered :

# THE LONELY HEART

*He wants not friends that hath Thy love,*
*And may converse and walk with Thee,*
*And with Thy saints here and above,*
*With whom for ever I must be.*

*In the communion of the saints*
*Is wisdom, safety and delight;*
*And, when my heart declines and faints,*
*It's raisèd by their heat and light!*

*Before Thy throne we daily meet,*
*As joint petitioners to Thee;*
*In spirit we each other greet,*
*And shall again each other see.*

*The heavenly hosts, world without end,*
*Shall be my company above;*
*And Thou, my best and surest Friend,*
*Who shall divide me from Thy love?*

## 15

# When We Are Set Apart

*To get alone—to dare to be alone—with God, this, I am persuaded, is one of the best ways of doing anything in the world.*

FORBES ROBINSON

IN a previous chapter I have mentioned Professor Bouman's study of our era entitled *Revolution of the Lonely*. Much of the destruction and upheaval of the last fifty years, says this distinguished sociologist, can be traced back to loneliness at the heart of masses of the people, and to the nihilism of their leaders. He provides vivid pen-pictures of those whose gathering isolation twice in these years brought the nations to the brink of destruction. But he also writes of others who took a different course, who made their solitariness yield rich dividends, accruing not only to their own benefit but to that of multitudes of others. Folk like Madame Curie, Tolstoy, Gandhi, Schweitzer and Kagawa turned what in them and about them was set apart into a fountain for creativity and deeds of love and mercy. Indeed, says Prof. Bouman, "There are forms of loneliness which are a prerequisite of all mental creation and for all works of charity. In this sense, Schweitzer felt himself united to Tolstoy, Rilke, Curie and many others who were conscious of the ministering function of their loneliness."[1] These people were able to use their solitariness in a positive, constructive fashion.

[1] *Revolution of the Lonely* (McGraw Hill), p. 152. Quoted by kind permission.

123

In Volume III of his great *Study of History,* Prof. Arnold Toynbee has a fascinating section in which he analyses the qualities requisite in the leaders who renew the course of history from time to time and who prevent civilizations from going moribund. In the lives of these men he sees a pattern of withdrawal and return. Before fulfilling their destiny they must first discover their powers and come to a sense of mission. This happens in the period of withdrawal. It is an astonishing list of examples that Toynbee adduces in support of his argument, from Moses and our Lord to Lenin and Hindenburg!

"When it was the good pleasure of God," writes St. Paul in his letter to the Galatians, "to reveal his Son in me, that I might preach him among the Gentiles; immediately I conferred not with flesh and blood . . . but I went away into Arabia." It was those three years in Arabia, as well as the later years of withdrawal in Tarsus that helped to fashion Paul into the flaming apostle that he became. Ghandi's life bears similar interpretation. It was his time of ostracism and imprisonment in South Africa that developed him. From those months of enforced solitude he emerged with a new power—*satyagraha,* soul-force. He possessed it in himself, and was able to persuade other people to experiment with it. By means of it later he achieved the bloodless revolution by which India passed from the British Raj to independence. Every time Ghandi was sent to prison he emerged a stronger man. It was the most foolish step his opponents took ever to put him in jail!

Artists, writers, musicians—creative people of every kind —have found the necessity for withdrawal and solitude. They need their studio, their study, their walk in the woods alone, having discovered that work demanding inspiration is impossible without time spent apart.

The saints have always known this.

Because of the power that can come to those who use solitude aright, the British philosopher, A. N. Whitehead, came to find here the focal point of religion. "There is no such thing as absolutely independent existence," he grants. "You cannot abstract society from man. . . . But all collective emotions leave untouched the awful ultimate fact, which is the human being, consciously alone with itself, for its own sake."

"Religion," he wrote, "is what the individual does with his own solitariness." By means of it he finds his way through to God. "Thus religion," he continues, "is solitariness; and if you are never solitary, you are never religious."[1] There is a fascinating picture afforded in a letter Edward Wilson wrote to his wife on January 4th, 1911, while journeying with Captain Scott towards the Pole. Wilson was the ship's artist as well as her doctor. Later, he was one of that heroic band who died with Scott in the cold wastes of Antarctica.

From shipboard we find him writing: "I simply love the Crow's Nest—my private chapel. I have spent the happiest times you can possibly imagine there . . . alone with God and with you." He gives us a stirring glimpse of a man finding seclusion near the top of a ship's mast. With the sky above him, and miles of ice-packed sea below, his restricted position prevented him from sketching though others thought that it was for that very purpose that he spent so much time there.

All of us need a private chapel of some kind. One of the difficulties is where to find it. We need time to think things out, and a place where we can keep our communion fresh with God. We need the space and freedom that meditation brings so that our souls can breathe. Always hemmed in by other people, there is a part of our nature which cannot find expression until we are alone. "There are tracts in my life," confessed Rabindranath Tagore, "that are bare and silent. They are the open spaces where my busy days had their light and air."

[1] *Religion in the Making:* Cambridge Univ. Press, pp. 6 f.

Our Lord, in the crowded days of His ministry, sought opportunities for quiet. His custom seems to have been to find some secluded spot on the mountainside for communion with His Father. "And in the morning, rising up a great while before day, He went out, and departed into a solitary place, and there prayed." (Mark 1 : 35.) His disciples found Him there. "All men seek for Thee," they reported. It was *because* of crowds, as well as for His own soul's sake, that Jesus required these precious moments alone, away from people and their claims—moments of communion, prayer, and refreshment in God. From them He could return to serve others better.

Before He began His ministry He needed a long period alone in which to think things through. I often wonder, when He went down to Jordan to be baptised, whether He knew that this was the end of one phase of His life and the beginning of another. There are those who are sure that when He shut the door of the carpenter's shop, He knew He had done so for the last time. I am not so confident. What is certain is that He had determined to identify Himself completely with this movement of preparation under John. As a sign of His own readiness for whatever God wanted, or offered in His coming Kingdom, He presented Himself for baptism. *Then* there came to Him the sign. He knew God's acceptance of Him, knew that the Spirit was upon Him in power. He was to be the One in whom the Kingdom came.

It is Mark who tells us "Straightway the Spirit driveth Him into the wilderness to be tempted of the devil forty days." Matthew and Luke enlarge the story with details that could only have come from Jesus. I have referred before to the fact that our Lord was willing to admit that He was put to the test in this way. Here I draw attention to the nature of these tests. Alone in the desert He faced the challenge of the future, thinking through His campaign and His mission, coming to realise a little of what it

would mean to lead the life of the Son of God in a material-
istic world. The form of the temptations makes this clear:
"If thou be the Son of God," then . . . why not do this or
that? You have unlimited power, why not use it in ways
that will bring quick returns?

It seems to have been the Lord's habit to consider carefully all the tests of His ministry before entering them.
This He did in quiet and prayer before they occurred.
It is worth noting the hints in the Gospel story (especially
in Luke's account) that reveal this. Right at the beginning,
with this sense of commissioning upon Him and the knowledge of available power, He faced the implications of His
future ministry alone. Later, in Gethsemane, He was to
endure the agony of the Cross before He felt the touch of
the wood and the nails. I now return to the point in Mark's
summary of the Temptation story, that it was the Spirit
that drove Jesus into the wilderness. The power that was
upon Him guided Him out into the desert. In other words,
God set Him apart.

We need, then, to observe two points: (1) that it is wise
for us to secure time for quiet, away from the pressures of
life. The more we seek to serve God and others then the
more, and not the less, we need this. We must also notice
(2) that for our spiritual development it may be necessary
to pass through what might be called an anti-social phase.
So as to serve our fellows better we have to leave them
for a time. People who have experienced this know what
it is to be driven by the Spirit into the wilderness. God
is the power behind both these compelling impulses by
which we are set apart. We will look at them separately.

(1) "When thou prayest," Jesus advised the Pharisees,
"enter into thine inner chamber, and having shut thy
door, pray to thy Father which seeth in secret, and thy
Father which seeth in secret shall recompense thee openly."
There has been much discussion where in the house of
those days there was an inner chamber. A suggestion made

by Karl Heim, the German scholar, is that the *tameion* represented a cubby-hole, something like a modern pantry. You could go into it if you were sufficiently determined! Although surrounded by seeds and fruits, amidst the smell of oil and sour wine, by pulling the door shut you would at least be alone. In these words, then, Jesus is saying, you must find a means of securing solitude, even if you have to adopt unusual methods to obtain it.

I know a minister, brought up in the country, who lived and worked for thirty-five years in the heart of crowded London. He told me he accepted the work most unwillingly. But he went at the call of his Lord, and in love for the people of a needy slum area. Recently he told a group of us how through the years he had kept his soul alive. Westminster Bridge, he said, was for him a pipe-line of salvation. By crossing it, he could spend a few moments in busy St. James's Park, or walk alone along bustling London streets. In Regent Street, or Piccadilly, he said, one could be quite alone for the people hurrying by were all strangers. It was here, in these unlikely places, that he found his best opportunities for communion and solitude—in the very centre of London's noise and traffic. At one time he used to compose hymns—simple, straightforward verses in modern style. Many of these, he said, came to him while treading these crowded thoroughfares. One was written on a piece of paper held against the window of a large store.[1]

[1] Regarding the possibilities of seeking solitude, and the inspiration that it can give, amid the crowd itself, it is refreshing to find the novelist, Thomas Burke, confessing to the same thing. He found inspiration for his books out on the streets, walking and observing solitarily. He says that it is a false assumption that the man who likes city life is necessarily of gregarious nature. "It is just because I like solitude," he writes in his autobiography (*Living in Bloomsbury:* George Allen & Unwin, pp. 13, 16), "that I like London. In its continental spaces I can be alone. My experience of country life . . . is that one can never be sure of being alone. Wherever one goes, one is watched by villagers. . . . I like to move alone on the edge of the surge of Regent Street and the Strand. As the countryman, lonely among his

(2) In the course of spiritual development, the Spirit of God may drive a man or a woman apart for a season. This concerns not the need for specific times of quiet and prayer but the thrusting-out of certain people in what we have described as an anti-social phase. This period may lengthen into months, or even years.

Jack Clemo, a Cornish poet, has written two autobiographical books and a novel which help us to understand something of his spiritual pilgrimage. His has been a difficult journey. In *The Invading Gospel* he reveals that it was in spite of himself that God laid His hand upon him, invading him with grace, love, mercy and forgiveness in Christ. The way that this happened, and the conclusions to which Clemo came, make his books a record of first-hand religious experience which both thrill and infuriate.

Jack Clemo is one who went through a phase similar to what we are discussing. He had to find God and be found of Him by himself, apart from others. Out on the clay dumps, away from the chapels, he would spend his time, reading his Bible, praying and meditating, and even storming at God. Only later did he find his way back into the life of the Cornish chapels from which he had come. The path he had to travel will not be that for many others—we are not all poets, nor have we the strange background of a Jack Clemo. But it was unquestionably the way for him.

In his book so rightly called *Confessions of a Rebel,* Clemo is scathing about those who accuse the Church of not being progressive enough for modern youth, and who blandly assert that youth has turned away from the Church because of her aloofness and because she has failed to adapt herself to social reform and scientific thinking. For him the facts were completely the reverse. "For me," he says,

---

hills, feels a sense of oneness with the earth, so, on the fringe of the crowd, I feel a sense of oneness with my unknown fellows. I have often been alone in London. I have never been lonely."

"I knew there was no room in a church that made no provision for this initial anti-social phase of Christian experience, a church which, though founded to be the channel of that mystical disruptive power, was actually embarrassed when the power broke through its superficial routine and isolated a soul in naked spiritual vision."[1]

Those called to leadership in the Church need to watch more carefully. We should notice what God is doing with some of our young people. Instead of feeling that we must draw them into meetings, we need to recognize that sometimes the very opposite is what is required for a time. We are so sure that the Church exists for fellowship that we fail to realise that to bring some people into the fellowship, they must first be set apart!

Centuries ago, God did that with George Fox. His parents wanted him to become an orthodox minister. But this lover of people whom God used to build up the Society of Friends, found that he, too, was driven by the Spirit into the wilderness. It was a most uncomfortable process. Here is the account from his *Journal* of the time when he was 22–23 years of age: "But my troubles continued, and I was often under great temptations; I fasted much, and walked abroad in solitary places many days, and often took my Bible, and went and sat in hollow trees and lonesome places till night came on; and frequently, in the night, walked mournfully about by myself: for I was a man of sorrows in the times of the first working of the Lord in me."

\* \* \* \* \*

There is another point that needs to be made. Some seek solitude, as did the Lord Himself, for the sake of communion. Others, especially in times of awakening and conversion, must endure an anti-social phase of religion. But there are others set aside by disability or illness. Many

[1] Quoted from *Confessions of a Rebel* (Chatto & Windus) by kind permission of Messrs. A. M. Heath & Co. Ltd., agents for Jack Clemo.

of these have been able to turn physical disadvantage to good account.

Some years ago I was the minister of a thriving church. Part of its secret, I am now sure, lay in the fact that we had two women of utterly different temperament who were united in this. Invalided as they were, they shared a common concern for the church and were women of prayer. Everything that we did was undergirded by their prayers and interest. I believe that they did more for that church than any of us who were endlessly bustling about its premises.

Insights are possible to the "shut-ins" and the "shut-aways" that never come to us. They have time to discover the Kingdom within. They have a chance to be themselves. There is no public stage on which they have to strut. For them no subterfuge is necessary. Nor is force of mass opinion so likely to overcome them.

In one of her letters to her husband, Middleton Murry, Katherine Mansfield wrote: "Perhaps loneliness is not the terrible thing we believe it to be. Perhaps achievement begins at the point where we have changed it from a negative to a positive state, from a barren to a pregnant." At the time she wrote these words she was suffering from a consumption which later proved fatal.

There is a record of an occasion when C. F. Andrews, towards the end of his life, spoke to a group of young Indians. He told them of the time when he had worked among the poor in South London, taking scarcely any time off for rest, and finding little time for quiet and prayer. Then at the age of thirty-four, when he arrived in India, he was rebuked by the peace which so many people seemed to possess. Men like Rudra, Sadhu Sundar Singh, and Tagore became his friends. From them he learned something of the true meaning of peace within.

"But," he said, "I think the greatest of all lessons which I learnt was through illness." He was referring to the time when he contracted cholera, and was nursed by no less a person than Rabindranath Tagore himself at his Ashram at Santiniketan. For many weeks he lay at death's door. "In that time," said C. F. Andrews, "I had my own simple and tender teaching from God Himself."[1] He had found the silent way to inner communion with God. Being laid aside resulted in learning a lesson which meant more to him than anything else.

Here is the "pearl of great price, which is worth all the rest of the treasures of life put together". Here loneliness is not just a pathetic thing, bravely endured. Solitude itself can be found to be rewarding and full of blessing, because in the silence of our inner being we have now found Christ.

[1] Quoted with permission from an appendix on pp. 112 ff. of *The Inner Life* by C. F. Andrews, published in 1939 by Messrs. Hodder & Stoughton Ltd., of London.

**16**

# Breaking the Vicious Circle

*No man is an island, entire of itself, every man is a
piece of the continent, a part of the main.*

JOHN DONNE

UNDERLYING so much of the world's trouble is a
second tragedy—that much of it is unnecessary.
Especially is this true of loneliness. What is required
from many who daily endure its agony is only a little
of the spirit of adventure, a little outgoing from the inner
citadel of one's own nature, a little genuine love springing
forth. The loneliness that is such a nightmare would
then vanish like shadows before the morning sun.

A reply Jesus once gave to a request says much to us
about our subject. His disciples had seen something wonderfully at work in Him, and were very conscious, at the
same time, of its lack in them. So they asked Him to help.
"Lord," they cried, "increase our faith." Here is His reply
—a reply which on the first hearing seems almost irrele-
vant: "If you had faith as a grain of mustard seed, you
would say unto this sycamine tree be thou rooted up and
planted in the sea, and it would obey you."

The reference to the tree planted in the sea is in the
language of Eastern metaphor and exaggeration, and is not
our concern here. What we must notice, however, is the
way in which our Lord throws back the disciples' request.
"If you have . . . you would say . . ." He is telling them
that the answer they seek is not in any magical augmenta-
tion of their faith. They themselves possess the key. Faith

grows by exercise. Use what you have of it! Even if it seems as tiny as a grain of mustard seed. From our Lord's employment of this expression elsewhere we know that He is thinking of faith as a lively, developing thing. A mustard seed may be tiny, but it grows into a big plant. Use what you have! Start now! That is the way to increase any spiritual power.

To those wanting to break out of the vicious circle of loneliness there comes an echo of this best of advice: use what you have now. Adventure with that little you already possess of the spirit of love and camaraderie *now*. By this is meant much more than an exhortation to "Shake yourself out of your depression", or "Get out and get among people". Lonely folk have been told this too many times already. But we must start with recommendations that look very similiar: be ready to adventure; be ready to use what social gifts and social charm you possess. Even if you think you have none—then be willing to start out with what love you can discover. It may seem but a tiny grain, smaller even than a mustard seed. Never mind. It is enough. The Master says so.

So many people need not be lonely. In Hugh l'Anson Fausset's phrase, they are standing in their own light and wondering why it is dark. There is a way into the light for all.

Think, for instance, of the folk who long for friendship, who want to be loved and appreciated, but who will never give love—or anything else—themselves. They seem tied-up in their inner nature. Now the law of the mustard seed works in two ways. It is true that powers grow by use. It is equally true that unused powers wither. "To him that hath shall be given," said Jesus, "and from him that hath not shall be taken away even that which he hath." These folk had better transfer therefore to the *positive* side of the law's outworking. If we have unconsciously been practising the technique of withdrawing from people, of which Karen Horney wrote, we must realise that to reverse this process after many years is not going to be easy.

Previous attempts to achieve good relationships with others may have left us discouraged. This happens to a number of people. Some disguise their sense of failure by assuming a dignified aloofness. Most of our poor attempts to make contact with others, we need to know, are not to be explained entirely by reference to our present situation and condition—they go back to situations long forgotten. Failure in this matter started in us a vicious circle years ago. Now we mean to reverse this. The first step is to recognize past failures, and plan future strategy on that basis.

In her book *Understanding Fear,* Bonaro W. Overstreet quotes two lines of James Stephens':

*All songs of escape from love are songs of despair*
*Who hath so gat him away hath gat nowhere.*

With much truth she goes on to comment, "Not only all *songs* of escape from love are expressive of despair, but so are all *actions* that are a retreat from love and learning."

Right then! From this moment onward we cease to retreat. There is to be no more escaping from love and its demands. Instead, we must learn how to express it; to thaw, even if it be by ever so little. Emerson's oft-quoted sentence will be a guide: "He who wants friends must show himself friendly."

Earlier we spoke of the many strokes of genius behind the Alcoholics Anonymous movement. One of them is the teaching of a day-to-day philosophy. The reclaimed alcoholic is usually in a tremendous hurry to right the wrongs of a lifetime. The wise plan is to do the utmost just for the day ahead. His mental and spiritual capital is so small that he is unwise to pledge it for the rest of his life. All

he needs to do is to pledge himself for the twenty-four
hours ahead. That is far enough. For tomorrow, he can
repeat the process. Let us follow this wise policy; and perhaps mingle it with that advocated by the late Lord Baden
Powell. A scout sets himself to do at least one good deed
a day. There is no limit but the operative idea is *at least
one* good deed a day. So let us set ourselves this kind of
simple target: that we will allow ourselves to thaw *this
day*: that we will smile at others *today*: that during these
twenty-four hours we will do at least one loving deed. We
want to be loved. We will set ourselves to be loving and
kind for the hours immediately ahead. Then tomorrow
we can renew our determination, and find that we are
forging a new way of living. We are out of the dark for
good.

\* \* \* \* \*

In considering this problem of disengaging ourselves
from loneliness, we must bear in mind a point to which
we have continually returned. A real distance needs to be
established between the closest of human beings. All of
us require privacy and solitude. These are elements in our
nature not to be neglected, but safeguarded. Nothing that
we have said about reducing loneliness should be misunderstood as an invitation to give up privacy. If,
however, we are among the lonely it may be that we
have kept a further distance from others than we ought,
and for that reason have never been able to establish
the contact that we should. What is needed is some way
of getting *a little* nearer. That is all. Then we are in
touch.

I remember Dr. E. Graham Howe describing this ambi-
valence in our nature by which we need both fellowship
and solitude, friendship and privacy. He said we are like
islands, and rightly so, for we have personal identity and
sovereign independence. But we are "islands that like to
be visited". Said he, we must respect the space that separ-

ates us. It is important that we should, both for ourselves and for one another. But this space is not a negative thing. It is important because though separating it also unites us.

Matthew Arnold felt this separation from others very strongly. In his poem *Isolation* he uses this same metaphor of islands and sea.

> *Yes: in the sea of life en-isled,*
> *With echoing straits between us thrown,*
> *Dotting the shoreless watery wild,*
> *We mortal millions live* alone.
> *The islands feel the enclasping flow,*
> *And then their endless bounds they know.*

In the last verse he asserts that the severance between us is in fact due to the dispensation of "a God". He failed to grasp that there is more than that. When each of us discovers the undergirding fact behind all our lives, our personal relationship with God, a new kind of unity and union is established.

Another aspect of the truth after which we are now groping is that God is not now the One whom we describe only as THOU. He establishes a relationship that develops *within us*. God is the one invader of the central citadel of our soul that need not, and must not, be kept at a distance. To keep Him at bay involves us in the basic loneliness from which all other facets develop. He is the uniting force behind all our lives.

Our Lord told us to love God and to love our neighbour as ourselves. He underlined and reinforced these Old Testament precepts. On them, He said, all real religion depends, all real living, too. Now notice: the lonely person fails *at all* three points. He neither loves God with heart and soul and mind and strength, nor his neighbour, nor even himself.

Those who knew that remarkable man, Lawrence of Arabia, discovered in him a fatal flaw. He was not really interested in other people. He supplies the reason himself. "Indeed," he writes, "I did not like the 'myself' I could see and hear." We cannot love our neighbour properly until we come to terms with ourselves. The isolated man's inability to be at peace with himself is often shown in the strangest of ways—even in what seems to be the opposite of loneliness: the desire to be among people, always with the crowd. For a person in this state, solitude is the thing most to be dreaded. The trouble is that only when we are caught *alone* do we have the opportunity to set things right.

The need is to break what we have called the vicious circle. To do this we must recognize love, and enter into it, *at some point*. To repeat the metaphor with which we began this chapter, we need to find and use our grain of mustard seed. What bit of love have we already in our nature—for God, for neighbours, and for others? Let us discover it, recognize it, and then invest it quickly.

The *commandment* that comes from our Lord is that we must move from ingrowing isolation to outgoing responsiveness. He does not argue with us, nor plead with us. He commands us to love.

Perhaps one of the best ways to break out from the circle of our in-growing defeat is to experiment with prayer. If we pray aright for others, helpfully and positively, we cannot fail to bless them. As they will be unaware of our effort, we shall have done something unselfish. One thing is certain: praying will make for easier relations between us and the folk for whom we pray.

I have written elsewhere of the great example of Forbes Robinson in the matter of praying for others.[1] Recommending the practice to a friend he wrote, "Just try to

[1] *Secrets of Answered Prayer,* published by Arthur James Ltd., Evesham, Worcs.

pray for some one person . . . and you will begin really to love him. . . . As you lay his life before God, as you pray earnestly for him . . . at the end of the time you will feel more interested in him. You enter then into another man's ego. You see him in God. You see him as an end in himself. Such praying takes you out of your own ego and links you, as well as the other person, with God."

## Part III

# Loneliness and God

*In loneliness, Lord, help me not to feel alone. Let me rejoice in the loving companionship of the invisible host by which I am spiritually encompassed. When I long for the touch of a vanished hand, give me a sense of love that never dies nor forgets. When I yearn for the sound of a voice that is still, speak Thou to me in Thy Word. Thou, O Divine Shepherd, dost companion me in the valley of the shadow, and lead me rejoicingly through quiet pastures and by the waters of stillness. Only in my blindness do I seem to be alone. Amen.*

C. A. HALL

# Part III

# Loneliness and God

**17**

# God Who Brings the Lonely Home

*You know always in your heart that you need God
more than you need everything: but do you not know
that God needs you—in the fullness of His eternity needs
you?*

MARTIN BUBER

IN his Negro Sermons, *God's Trombones*, James Weldon
Johnson, following the Genesis story, pictures God at
work in the processes of creation and dares to impute
motives to Him.

> *And God stepped out on space,*
> *And He looked around and said,*
> "I'm lonely—
> I'll make me a world...."[1]

As one great stroke of creation followed another, "That's
good," said God. But after them all He was lonely still.
Then He made clay out of the dust of the earth and
breathed into it the breath of life. And man became a
living soul. God had created a being capable of fellowship
with Him.

We do not know what God's motives were, nor would
we necessarily have any right to think of ourselves as of
any importance in the total scheme of things were it not
for two things. The whole panorama of Bible story and

[1] *God's Trombones* is published by George Allen & Unwin, London,
and by the Viking Press, New York.

revelation and our own experience speak to us of God's concern and interest in man. He desires that we should enter into fellowship with Him. We know, too, that we on our part are like lost children until we find ourselves in relationship with our heavenly Father. Here is our true destiny.

Martin Buber, the Jewish philosopher and theologian, has written of the way our experience of life passes through various stages. Our first knowledge, by which we are able to manage things at all, is of the world of I and It. By means of this we learn to recognize and manipulate the things about us. A great step forward comes with the recognition of persons. They confront us and stand over against us in their own right. (While we still live in the world of I and It even the persons with whom we deal are really things —we are trying to use them.) The new realm is the world of I and Thou. And the final encounter, says Buber, setting all other relationships right, is that with God, whom we come to know as THOU. This is the way to know God. We are face to face with Him, not trying to use Him, as a thing; nor thinking of Him as "It" nor even as "He". We now know Him—and everything else because of this—in a new way. "I have heard of Thee with the hearing of the ear," said Job, "but now mine eye seeth Thee."

This relationship of direct encounter is the one which God is concerned for us to discover. Life has a way of blinding us to it. We spend much of our time evading God instead of seeking Him. Sin and ignorance form palpable barriers keeping us from Him. The Bible unfolds the story of how man over and over again loses contact with God, and of the way that God sets about restoring it.

A golden phrase comes from Moffatt's translation of Psalm 68. The Psalmist is rejoicing in God's goodness to Israel and recounting the way He has brought His people out of captivity and exile. He tells the people to sing and exult in:

*the God who brings the lonely home,*
*and frees the prisoner for prosperity—*
*only the rebels have to live forlorn.*

In verses five and six the God enthroned in the heavens, who has so wonderfully blessed Israel, is revealed as caring for the lonely, the orphaned and the oppressed.

Dr. Moffatt's translation brings a truth to light applying not just to Jews but to all who have faith in God. He is at work, as Paul puts it, "reconciling the world unto Himself". This activity is seen supremely in Christ, in His Life, Death and Resurrection. These are now facts of history used by the living Spirit of God as points of power to "bring the lonely home". It is breathtaking to watch the many ways in which God is doing this in our own time. Let us look at the empty lives of two men, beginning to feel the misery of life in the "far country", who were fortunately brought home into a renewed relationship.

The first was a successful commercial traveller. His was the kind of success, however, that was taking him further and further along the road to personal disaster. By now, most of his contacts were made in the bars of public houses and hotels. He was fast becoming the person who provides the money but stays with the family, with rather bad grace, for only a night or two at a time. The church rarely saw any member of the family.

Then God took a hand. Arriving in a Midland town our friend stayed at a newly-opened commercial hotel. His room was small, with the minimum of fittings and furniture. On the polished top of the dressing-table was a brown-covered book. That was new too. He fingered it—a Bible. It was a "Gideon's Bible", placed by a group of dedicated Christians in hotels that would accept them.

Before he put the Book down, his eye was caught by a page at the beginning. The Gideons had set out their reasons for making the gift, hoping that the Bible would be used by travellers. Some passages were suggested for reading . . . if ill . . . if discouraged . . . if lonely.

It was the last suggestion that caught David's eye. Few of his business acquaintances would have suspected him of being lonely, yet that was just how he felt. Whilst driving through depressing industrial areas that very afternoon he had become overwhelmed with self-pity. He realised for the first time that he had no real friend. And so with a glimmer of interest he turned to one of the Bible passages which were suggested as an antidote. Perhaps—who knows?—there might be some message for him.

For years everything associated with the Bible had been dismissed by David with one word: "Bunk". No doubt these texts would be sentimental and unreal, suggesting completely impracticable ways of living. These cynical thoughts passed through his mind as he flicked over the pages. He paused. "I will never leave thee, nor forsake thee." Who made such promises? For years he had not been in the least aware of such a Presence. . . . Bunk!

He closed the Bible with a snap but curiously the words of the text persisted. They were in his mind through an evening of hard drinking. They were with him when he crawled into bed. Sleep would not come. Then he found himself thinking of his mother, whom he had rather neglected of late. "Now if anyone has a right to be called lonely," her son was thinking, "she has. My life is full compared with hers. And I haven't done much to help her lately."

Almost the first thing he said to his wife on his return was, "I must go and see Mother." He wrote a letter telling her he was coming for the week-end.

"Wouldn't you like to go to the service at the chapel?" his mother suggested on the Sunday morning. For old times' sake he thought he would. Some of the folk would be surprised to see him there!

There was nothing in the service that moved or gripped

him. The hymns were dull, the parson colourless. He found himself watching the faces and antics of two restless children. Of what was done or said during most of the service, David says, he had little idea until God spoke to him through a verse quoted by the parson:

> *Ships sail East and ships sail West,*
> *Wherever the winds may blow,*
> *For it's the set of the sails,*
> *And not the gales,*
> *That determine the way we go.*

Drifting—that is what he had been doing for years. His life was not worth living: he had set no course. That was why it was so empty: no real friends, merely acquaintances: no true fellowship: no love, at home or in business. He was just drifting with the wind.

> *It's the set of the sails*
> *And not the gales*
> *That determine the way we go.*

Sitting quietly in the back pew of the old church that memorable Sunday morning, David Dewars determined he would take a hand in setting his sails. Then into his thoughts came the verse he had read in the Gideon's Bible, "I will never leave thee, nor forsake thee". Perhaps, after all, that was true. Why not try it? He did!

At first he lived in a strange state of suppressed excitement and calm determination. Then bombshell after bombshell exploded. "I'm going to resign from my firm. I'm going to start again from scratch." Income fell almost to zero, as the climb from the bottom began. The old contacts were severed, but new ones helped him in his new way of life. He now thought of people differently, saw his work in a different light. All was changed. His family, though puzzled, tried their best to understand, for they liked the new person who was emerging.

How physically hard those early days were no one will know. But all the time there was Someone there, a Power to share the hard endeavour and adventure. Misery and self-pity disappeared. "I will never leave thee, nor forsake thee." It was true. At last he came to realise that this was the truth on which his mother's happy life had been based through her lonely years.

\*     \*     \*     \*     \*

The name of Julian Duguid, explorer and writer, will be familiar to many. He has been a frequent broadcaster, relating some of his adventures on the Amazon and throughout South America. In 1941 he published a book outlining adventures of another kind. It is an unusual book, fresh, not theological in any academic way. It deals with his own spiritual growth.

As a young man he had been driven away from Christianity. He explains that his difficulties were due to the ineptitude of parsons, the lack of sincerity of the Church, the aftermath of Darwinism, and the pressure of other scientific and philosophical concepts. Many people to-day, because of the complete impersonality of the world revealed by factual science, have found great difficulty in holding to the idea of a personal God. Julian was one of them.

On his first visit to the New World Duguid tells how he met with a "small, lithe, tough-set man, very wiry and quick on his feet". This man influenced Duguid profoundly, not so much by what he said as by what he was in himself. He was none other than Wilfred Grenfell, the missionary doctor of Labrador. The aura of peace and strength surrounding Grenfell attracted him greatly.

Duguid was forced to take notice of this strange compelling power. He later recognized this same irresistible force in another friend. Yet, for three years Duguid could not find peace of soul nor a sense of certainty. Other people's witness to fellowship with a personal God could not convince him. He had to find out for himself.

Later, thoughts of suicide came into his mind. He confesses to this quite honestly. He felt a deep despair—a fundamental sense of loneliness. Then he tells how, after bleak months of spiritual struggle, one evening he was sitting alone in his study. The lights had not yet been switched on. "I was wondering," he writes, "how long I could endure. Of a sudden, a soundless voice broke through the gunfire in my brain. It spoke without passion but with urgency.

"'Ask,' it said, 'and it shall be given you.'"

"'Very well,' I replied in despair, 'if there is anything present which can answer, let it tell me this: How can I believe with honesty in a loving and personal God?'"

"At that moment my wife came in with a large bowl of chrysanthemums. She placed them on a table in the window, turned on the light and went out. An instant later," says Duguid, "my mind was filled with understanding and a peace beyond description. It was as if a sun had blazed up in my brain."

The personal God is often discovered through people. His love is revealed in their love. When we know what is our real need our eyes are opened to His presence and help. His power is there all the time, but we must make the contact. It takes only two to make a meeting; but two it must be. In the answer that came to Julian Duguid all the pieces seemed to dovetail perfectly. Even the flowers were somehow part of the pattern.

Here is his own comment: "It was as neat as a one-act play. I was sitting in a chair near the fire, asking with a deep despondency for a sign that something existed. My wife entered as on a cue, placed the bowl of flowers in the window, turned on the light and departed. I had nothing to do with her movements, which were familiar, almost instinctive. Yet, whether or not it was chance, an astonishing sequence was in motion. My prayer to an unknown God was answered inside two minutes by the one action on earth which could have satisfied me at the time. It had the rightness of brilliant planning."[1]

The answer that came to Duguid resolved his difficulties in a flash. Intuitively he realised the relationship between the immeasurable power behind the universe and the reality of a loving, personal God. He knew he had at last made contact with Him. "Whole ramparts of agnostic doctrine," he says, "crumbled with the pulling of that switch." There was no more despair in his heart, no more thought of suicide.

\* \* \* \* \*

These are two simple stories out of many that might be told of God bringing the lonely home. "He setteth the solitary in families" is the Authorised Version of this sixth verse of Psalm 68. God is able to deal faithfully, lovingly, healingly with the bruised people of the world. He should especially be able to do this from within the family of His people, which is His Church. Wherever there is a responsive and loving community, declaring His gospel and sharing His Spirit, this will always happen.

[1] These quotations are by permission from *I am Persuaded*, published in 1941 by Messrs. Jonathan Cape of London.

**18**

# The Loneliness of Christ

*I see now that the loneliness of God is His strength:*
*what would He be if He listened to your jealous little*
*counsels? Well, my loneliness shall be my strength too:*
*it is better to be alone with God. His Friendship will not*
*fail me, nor His counsel, nor His love. In His strength I*
*will dare, and dare and dare, until I die.*

St. Joan: BERNARD SHAW

IT is a wonderful thing to remember that the experience of
loneliness is something which the Lord Christ has shared.

He spoke to His disciples the words recorded in John
16: 32, "Behold the hour cometh, yea, is now come, that ye
shall be scattered, every man to his own, and shall leave me
alone: and yet I am not alone, because the Father is with
me." Jesus knew what it was to stand in a minority of one,
misunderstood and isolated.

His loneliness, however, was unique and beyond human
understanding. It did not come from introversion nor withdrawal. Its origins lay in another direction. The truth is
that no one less desired to be isolated than He. No one has
ever lived so fully in the spirit of love and affection, so
desirous for fellowship as Jesus. Mark tells us of the choos-
ing of the Twelve:—"He ordained twelve, that they should
be with Him. . . ." "Ye are they," He said in the same
Upper Room where He foretold their desertion, "which
have continued with me in my temptations." He had always
wanted them near—on the Mount of Transfiguration, and
in the Garden of Gethsemane. His whole ministry was

aimed at restoring the severed relationships between man and God, thereby enabling man to love and serve his fellows. The tragic fact is that in the tremendous effort of fulfilling this very purpose—in the interests of reconciliation and eternal friendship—He came to tread the path of supreme loneliness.

All great leaders must know a certain isolation. They wish others to follow: but their position, out in front, is a lonely one. St. Francis came to this tragic discovery. He who loved men so deeply found that there were occasions when, for God's sake, he had to pursue his vision alone. In John Drinkwater's play, *Abraham Lincoln,* we are made to feel the unshared greatness of "Honest Abe". Surrounded by smaller men, misunderstanding his motives and not prepared to accept his vision, he, too, had to forge ahead alone. During his last months, ex-President Wilson knew a tragic isolation, with his countrymen refusing to follow the lead he had given towards founding a League of Nations.

All who live on the heights experience this. It is one of the penalties of leadership. But there has never been a peak like the one Jesus scaled, nor a journey more misunderstood. The records of His ministry reveal the distance separating Him from His followers. They followed, it is true, but often blindly and pathetically, not realising what was the Driving Force. His mother and His brethren understood Him even less. In Mark's realistic account we are told of the time when they said He was "beside Himself" which suggests, from the human standpoint, He was acting in an irrational manner.

In 1882 Henrik Ibsen wrote *An Enemy of the People.* He describes a doctor faithful to his unacceptable findings even when they earned him the title of "an enemy of the people". It is to be noted that the doctor was driven into isolation because of his integrity. He retained the loyalty of his family, however. But for most of His ministry Jesus had not even the understanding of "His own". Our loving Lord warns us: "A man's foes shall be they of his own household." He knew for Himself that bitter experience.

When the hour of the Cross was at hand those whom He had chosen did as He had foretold: they forsook Him and fled, leaving Him alone to face His enemies.

As He knew, His ministry had now brought Him to complete isolation: only the Father was with Him. It was His dark hour. He was the One revealing God's plan; in Him the Kingdom had come; through Him God was breaking down and overcoming the barriers that prevented the fulfilment of that Kingdom. The greatest of these barriers was human discord with God—which theologians call sin. The vital issue in connection with this had to be contested. Sin had to be defeated. It was indeed a battle to the death!

On the Cross man's sin is both exposed and absorbed. As we see Jesus there we are reminded that *this* is what human sin can do to the Loveliest and the Best. *This* is how humanity receives God. The meaning and the power of the Cross stretches right through time, and we today share the blame and cost with those who actually caused Him to die this shameful death. "Were you there when they crucified my Lord?" We know that in a certain sense we were.

Christ "bore man's sin on the Cross" knowing that final victory would be His. He went voluntarily to His Death, neither fleeing from it, nor using His divine powers to evade its horror. "He who knew no sin became sin for us" is the graphic way Paul describes the truth behind this selfless act. In the moment of His Death He identified Himself with our struggle. From the Cross God's love and God's forgiveness are manifested as surely as man's sin is there exposed.

F. W. Faber has a verse which takes us to the heart of the matter:

> *O Love of God! O sin of man!*
> *In this dread act your strength is tried;*
> *And victory remains with love;*
> *For He, our Lord, is crucified.*

By allowing sin full expression, by tasting death and humiliation, Jesus went through the gate of defeat to final triumph. The very forces that by His Death seemed to have conquered were there confounded. The story of Cross and Resurrection are one. The triumph is not an addendum!

This was the loneliest venture the world has ever witnessed. No one living in the world at that time, save the Lord Himself, saw the least sense in it. It looked like the end. Even Jesus Himself endured it seemingly in blind faith—conscious only that it was His Father's will to which He committed Himself unreservedly.

It is out of this shattering experience we hear the agonising cry: "My God, my God, why hast Thou forsaken me?" When He uttered this "cry of dereliction" Jesus was truly in the pit of loneliness. Here He was encountering something He had never met before. Until then His life had been uninterrupted communion with the Father. Now, as He tastes sin and death for every man, He knows what it is to feel cast off and forsaken. Here was loneliness indeed!

\* \* \* \* \*

In the year 1870 a young disciple of Jesus landed in China as a missionary of the London Missionary Society, preaching this very message of the Cross. In those dangerous days he made his way into the hinterland to attempt, single-handed, the evangelisation of Mongolia! This enormous region is inhabited by wandering nomads all devoutly Buddhist. In that bleak and inhospitable climate life was of the most primitive character, and James Gilmour, this young Scot, who began with such sanguine aspirations, continued to work there for twenty long years. It is an extraordinary story of missionary endeavour and fortitude.

His diary tells of his first attempts to learn the language of this strange people and to get close to them. One entry mentions his extreme loneliness. It continues, "Today I felt a good deal like Elijah in the wilderness. . . . He prayed that he might die. I wonder if I am telling the truth when I say that I felt strongly drawn towards suicide. I take this opportunity of declaring emphatically that on all occasions two missionaries should go together. I was not of this opinion a few weeks ago, but I had no idea of how weak an individual I am. My eyes have filled with tears frequently these last few days in spite of myself, and I do not wonder in the least that one of the traders out here shot himself. *Oh! the intense loneliness of Christ's life,* not a single one understood Him! He bore it. O Jesus, let me follow in Thy steps, and have in me the same Spirit that Thou hadst!"

Throughout the centuries Christ's soldiers when sorely tested have found strength in remembering His endurance. Still more they have found help in the fact of His Presence.

In recent troubled times Bishop Lajos Ordass of the Lutheran Church in Hungary was imprisoned on a trumped-up charge. When released he said to a crowded Budapest church: "When everybody deserted me and I shook with fear, my Saviour called me and took me in His strong arms. He led me through a burning flame and showed me the beginning of a new life."

Our Saviour endured the Cross and knew its infinite and terrible loneliness. It is true that "He felt forsaken that we might know that we should never be forsaken". Wherever we go He is with us: we have but to turn in our hour of need.

> *Lord, should fear and anguish roll*
> *Darkly o'er my sinful soul,*
> *Thou, who once was so bereft*
> *That Thine own might ne'er be left,*
> *Teach me by that bitter cry*
> *In the gloom to know Thee nigh.*[1]

[1] John Ellerton.

**19**

# The Comforter

*You need not cry very loud: He is nearer to us than we think.*

BROTHER LAWRENCE

IN the Upper Room on the night of His Betrayal, Jesus warned His disciples of what lay ahead and tried to prepare them for the stresses to which they would be subjected. He spoke of His departure and of the Comforter whom the Father would send in His name. The disciples must have listened bewildered. How could He both be leaving and yet be with them? How could it be "expedient for them" that He should go away? That was the mystery.

The meaning of these words was unfolded in startling clarity as the events of the Cross, Resurrection and Ascension followed one another. At Pentecost, they knew the invasion of the Spirit. It was *then* that they experienced the Presence of the Comforter, and realised what Jesus had proclaimed in the Upper Room.

"I will not leave you comfortless: I will come to you," Jesus had said. The word that the Authorised Version translates as "comfortless" means, literally, "orphaned". The relationship with His disciples was such that breaking it left them fatherless indeed. Yet, as He promised, they soon discovered they were not alone. In a new and deeper way they felt His Presence with them in spirit.

These words of the Lord's contain a message for us in our day. It is not that we shall ever have to face leaving the man Jesus to discover fellowship with the spiritual Christ, for we can know Him only in spirit. What comes home to us with force, as we noticed at the end of the last chapter, is the truth that He will never forsake us. As Matthew records, "Lo, I am with you alway, even unto the end of the world."

Not everyone, alas, believes in these great promises. Many people, I suppose, regard this priceless promise of Christ as a scriptural quotation with little bearing on practical, everyday living. There are others who accept it in a vague way without experiencing its reality. "When I was a small boy," a man once wrote to me, "I used to sing a hymn with the chorus:

> *Yet never alone is the Christian*
> *Who lives by faith and prayer:*
> *For God is a friend unfailing*
> *And God is everywhere.*

"I am sorry to say," he went on, "that I always found these words terribly difficult to believe. I have never found it like this. Instead, at times of illness, hardship, trouble and perplexity, I have felt utterly and unutterably alone."

We must remember that temperament and disposition have an influence on spiritual matters as well as on material. Some find religion a much more intensely personal encounter than others. But whatever be the degree of our experience, it is still true that the heart of religion *is* personal. Only through ourselves and through contact in the realm within can we know the Presence of God.

It is not easy to sense this. The friend who wrote to me about his spiritual difficulties went on to say, "One sometimes wishes, fantastically, that some form of heavenly visitation were possible—an angel, perhaps, to chide and chastise us when we have done wrong—or to aid us when we need help! Anything rather than the 'voiceless void', the spiritual nothingness, that so often seems to confront us in hours of need." There *is*, of course, a certain barrenness about all things spiritual. This becomes apparent when we try to define what we mean by such words as "spirit" and "spiritual". The only things we can say with any confidence are largely negative—for spirit is the exact opposite to what is material, tangible and seen!

A host of witnesses, from St. Paul and St. Francis to David Livingstone and Bishop Ordass, declare, however, that they have proved the truth of Christ's promise and have lived, through dark times, in the certainty of it. Brother Lawrence has indeed introduced many people to the way of "practising the Presence", and Frank Laubach has modernized this into his "Game with Minutes".

The title that ex-Queen Wilhelmina of Holland chose for her memoirs is revealing. Translated into English it is *Lonely and Yet Not Alone*. Hers were fifty difficult years as Queen. The title reminds us—as does the book itself—how lonely rulership can be, and also how Queen as well as commoner can find relief from the same source—the guiding and sustaining presence of God.

It is a spiritual relationship that we share with Christ, but is nonetheless real. To those who will trust Him and go forward believing, there is a fund of dependability, a reservoir of love, and the background of a heart-warming relationship always renewed.

It may be that our relationship with Him has never gone very deep. If this be so then the truth of His promises cannot be known on such shallow terms. We must be prepared to accept full partnership and meet Him at all levels in daily living—emotional, intellectual, as well as spiritual. The watershed of John Wesley's experience in the upper room at Aldersgate Street stands as a reminder of the difference between mere intellectual belief and a deep spiritual faith, a religion of external performance and a religion of dynamic, personal character. "I felt I did trust in Christ, in Christ alone as my Saviour, and an assurance was given me that He had taken away my sins, even mine, and saved me from the law of sin and death. . . ." Something had invaded John Wesley. On the intellectual level he had not changed yet he knew he was a different man. He began immediately to pray for his enemies. A new spirit of love had entered his heart.

Thus the John Wesley who had once been keen, devoted, scholarly, but powerless, became the preacher of a personal religion that roused the dilettantes of his day. A clarion call was sounded in such texts as "The Spirit witnesseth with our spirits that we are children of God". The Wesley hymns are full of personal pronouns which still shock those whose religion knows nothing of this vital quality. The "Christian ethic", the "Christian philosophy", the "Christian way of life" are all impersonal abstractions. Martin Buber is right in his assertion that real religion begins elsewhere. It is a personal encounter expressed in the terms of I and THOU. It deepens when our frail lives are invaded by the Spirit and become vibrant with the power and love of God.

For some of the lonely to enjoy this experience they must first learn, paradoxically, to lose their loneliness in Him. So many are doing all they can to insulate themselves from Christ Jesus. They hug to themselves their spirit of self-sufficiency, or perversely enjoy their solitariness; and then wonder why He does not come. Our Lord spoke of barriers which must be dealt with before the power of God's Spirit and the fact of His forgiveness can flow into our lives. The unforgiving spirit is such a barrier. Pride is another, so is self-dependence. The man whose favourite phrase is, "I keep myself to myself" had better know that in doing so he will almost certainly keep himself away from Christ!

Dr. Stanley Jones, the veteran missionary, once stated, "I've never had a discouraged or lonely moment". That was after thirty-five years of travelling away from home. He tells[1]

---

[1] *Mastery*, p. 345 (Hodder & Stoughton, London; Abingdon Cokesbury, New York).

of a Chinese friend who journeyed with him during that time in America. The man's name was the shortest possible: it was Dr. Lo. One day when this Chinaman was feeling very miserable he turned the pages of his Bible and read, "Lo, I am with you alway." The promise could not have been more appropriate! He felt that with these words Christ was calling him by his own name, and reminding him of His continual Presence.

We ourselves can prove the truth of this promise. It is addressed to us personally if we accept Christ's commissioning and become His disciples. In the proving, however, we may find it difficult to differentiate between God in the way we speak of Him as Father, Son and Holy Spirit. These distinctions are points of theology and intellectual reasoning that disappear at the point of personal encounter. It is the One God whom we meet. We know Him now within ourselves.

> O strangely art Thou with us, Lord,
>     Neither in height nor depth to seek:
> In nearness shall Thy voice be heard;
>     Spirit to spirit Thou dost speak.

The mystery is solved in terms of our own experience. We know how Christ could promise His disciples that *He* would come again, and what it was to have *the Father* dwelling in them, and that the *Comforter*, the Holy Spirit, would be with them and in them. Within our being we know the living Presence of God, Who is One.

"It is expedient for you that I go away," Jesus announced in the Upper Room. Surely this "going away" would mean loss—of the very kind we have been discussing: loss of His personal Presence? They would have His teaching: that would remain. And the world would be richer for His influence and His life. But the world would not have *Him*. "I will send you," He goes on to promise in the teaching recorded in John, chapters 13–16, "another Comforter", and the word implies "another Strengthening Presence", an

Advocate, or Helper: a spiritual Presence who will take of the "things of Christ" and "apply" them to us. By Him the life of Jesus, His Death and Resurrection will be given new meaning and power, and become sources of life-giving and life-changing force. The Comforter will do that.

Further, the Comforter "shall be in you and with you" —the I and THOU in closest union!—bringing to our attention all that Jesus said, was and did. "He will witness to me." Thus the coming of the Spirit means not the invasion of some vague *dunamis,* but a Presence continuing all that Jesus began here on earth. Through the Spirit, we are linked with the Lord, the source of all power.

It becomes no longer a matter simply of "I and Thou" which, as we have said, takes us far into the heart of religion. It is "Thou in me" and "I in Thee", and "We" and "Us" "together in Him". For the One who invades us is the sharer of love and a source of unity between all who love and serve the Lord Jesus.

Here then is the answer to our loneliness: "I will not leave you comfortless, I come unto you". Into our secret inner selves comes the Holy Spirit, the Comforter. His home is in our hearts. The more we know of Him the more we know of the power of the Lord Jesus to liberate us, and of the power of the Spirit to draw us into fellowship with the others of Christ's flock.

> *Our heavenly Guide*
> *With us shall abide,*
> *His comforts impart,*
> *And set up His Kingdom of love in the heart.*

**20**

# The Rôle of the Church

*This is the bond of perfectness,*
*Thy spotless charity.*

CHARLES WESLEY

AS we come to the end of our survey the rôle of the Church in connection with loneliness is seen more clearly. The Church, as the body of believers gathered round Christ, empowered by the Spirit, and seeking to serve God the Father in actions both corporate and individual, has a unique commission to the lonely.

The Church is the agency set in the midst of the world continuing Christ's ministry, proclaiming His Gospel, and carrying the fact and the power of His victory to men, bringing them into the life of salvation. Whatever else the Church is, when she is true to herself she must always be the *proclaiming community*. She has this tremendous Gospel, the answer to man's hopes and needs. She can tell of the new life possible in Jesus, and can invite all men to share it. Never must it be forgotten that the power of the Spirit came upon the first disciples in order to make them effective *witnesses*. Part of the wonder of the story of the Day of Pentecost is that when the Spirit came, they started immediately on their new career by witnessing to Jesus in the inhospitable streets of Jerusalem.

The Church must not become in-growing. She has a mission to the world, which she neglects at her peril.

In Rudyard Kipling's autobiographical book, *Something of Myself*, he tells how after his marriage in 1892 he settled in a house which overlooked a wide valley in one of the loneliest stretches of New England. One spring day he and his wife made a journey to the far side. They were greeted by a hatchet-faced woman who lived in an isolated farmstead. "Be you the new lights 'crost the valley yonder?" she asked them fiercely. "Ye don't know what a comfort they've been to me this winter. Ye aren't ever goin' to shroud 'em up—or be ye?" As long as they lived there, Kipling said, the lights of their homestead were never "shrouded up". The memory of the meeting with their lonely neighbour was with them every time they lit their lamps. If only those of us in the Christian Church would realise how much our light is needed! If we knew just what it could mean, and ought to mean, to our neighbours we would not shroud our light as much as we do.

There is another point to remember in these days when many are critical and contemptuous or hold aloof from the Church: the power of the light she sheds not only depends on the quality and faithfulness of her members, but also on their numerical strength. It is never right to stand aside, to contract out of our responsibility for active witnessing within the community of Christ's people. We have each our part to play. The Church is the proclaiming community, and we share in her proclamation.

The Church is also *the fostering community*. She is the fold into which those who hear the message and respond are brought. She must provide discipline and training, and opportunities for quiet and solitude. In this sense her rôle is that of understanding and sheltering those who come within her influence. She should be building up their faith. She exists to share her priceless gifts in a caring community. Says H. A. Overstreet,[1] the psychologist and sociologist, the Church should be "*a place where love is*

---

[1] *The Great Enterprise*, p. 195, published by Victor Gollancz Ltd., London, and W. W. Norton & Co. Inc., New York. The italics are his. Quoted by kind permission.

*encouraged to grow by the sheer learning to like one
another and to be active in a common caring."*

Her officers are pastors, men with the shepherd heart.
Christ's words to Peter in John 21 were not, Can you batter
your way through opposition, or talk your head off in my
service? He asked, "Lovest thou me?" and then said, "Feed
my sheep", "Tend my lambs". This kind of Church would
be able to fulfil Jack Clemo's requirements—of waiting
and being ready to help a young member finding his way
through an anti-social phase of development, and would
be equally ready to give a warm welcome to others who
need another kind of approach. Always love, friendship
and understanding should be present.

"And he gave some, apostles; and some, prophets; and
some, evangelists; and some, pastors and teachers; for the
perfecting of the saints, for the work of the ministry, for
the edifying of the body of Christ," wrote Paul in
Ephesians 4: 11f. This ordaining to leadership and work is
so that the service (*diakonia*) of the Church shall be fulfilled and be all that it might be. The main idea behind
this word *diakonia,* as William Barclay reminds us, is
*practical service.* "The office-bearer," as he says, "is not
to be a man who simply talks and argues on matters of
theology and of Church law. He is in office to see that
practical service of God's poor and lonely people goes on."
We are emphasizing thus the third point: that the
Church is *the serving community.* By her nature she is
called to be this. Whether it be metaphor or fact that the
Church is the Body of Christ, under either heading it is
inescapable that the Church must exist to serve. We par-
take of the Body of Him who was, and is, the servant of all.

\*      \*      \*      \*      \*

Let us look at one or two examples of the Church
discharging her true rôle in the life of our day. These
examples show effects proceeding from a whole community,

from office-bearers and leaders, and sometimes more particularly from individual members.

First let us think of a man whose work belongs to our time, but who is no longer with us, and who cannot therefore be embarrassed by this mention. From one source and another I have heard a great deal about Don Robbins and his church. He was a big-built fellow, pilot in the First World War's Royal Flying Corps. Largely through the influence of another unique parson, Pat McCormick, this somewhat unusual man himself became a parson. Eventually he was appointed to St. George's, a down-town church in Leeds.

Paul Gliddon tells something of his story in a book that answers the question *But Who Was Don Robbins?* He was a parson convinced that the family was the pattern for all human society, including that of the Church. That was just what he wanted his church to be, and more and more, under his genial leadership, that was what it became. The crypt of St. George's, once a derelict rubbish heap, became a shelter for homeless men. The institute connected with the church was renamed "Friendship House" and the change of name was indicative of deeper change.

An insight into the kind of man Don Robbins was can be gained from one fact recorded by Paul Gliddon. "When he knew that people were especially lonely, or had struck a rather rough bit of road, he used to slip in towards the end of the evening just to call out 'Good-night'. Sometimes he would continue to do this for a couple of months on end, sometimes for a couple of years."[1]

After the Second World War, Don realised the loneliness of the prisoners of war left in Britain, and then of the displaced persons who arrived later. No trouble to improve their lonely state was too great for him. He also opened an Old Folks' Club for the elderly. I know a little of the way that nurses and doctors from Leeds Infirmary were

[1] Taken from *But Who was Don Robbins?* Published by James Clarke & Co. Ltd., London, and quoted by kind permission.

made to feel that there was a real home-from-home nearby.
Running parallel with all this splendid service was an
equally understanding evangelistic activity. We are told
that the worship of the church was such that prayerful
dedication was the focal point of every activity.

\*         \*         \*         \*         \*

It has never failed to impress me that for a number of
years the City Temple, in the heart of London, has been
especially concerned about a Ministry to the Lonely. The
variety of service that is possible is illustrated by the way
it engages in this activity. Dr. Leslie Weatherhead, who
has been its minister for twenty-five years, has always been
interested in psychiatric work. For many years ten medical
psychologists have assisted him in the City Temple Clinic.
How many lonely people they must have helped over the
years no one will ever know. More than that, in addition
to the church's many other agencies, they have pioneered
a form of fellowship meeting attended by folk under
psychiatric treatment. "Group therapy" is something
which has proved most valuable in helping people whose
lives have been twisted out of normal paths. This particular fellowship has encouraged many back to normality
and proved a place where loneliness has disappeared.

Recently the City Temple appointed as assistant to Dr.
Weatherhead, the Rev. Marjorie Inkster, a Congregational
minister. After working for the necessary degrees, Miss
Inkster served for a while as an R.A.F. Chaplain, then
took a course of psychiatric training to become a National
Health Psychiatric Worker. This brought her closely into
touch with lonely people. It made her certain that to deal
adequately with this complicated problem one needed the
extra dimension offered by religion. But in secular service
it is not always easy to introduce Christianity. Her work
at the City Temple now provides her with all the freedom
and facilities she requires. Many London newspapers were

interested in this appointment. Vincent Mulchrome wrote an article for the *Daily Mail* entitled *The Twilight Parish of Marjorie Inkster,* emphasising her work among the lonely. To quote from the article, she was "to pioneer a ministry in Britain's strangest 'parish', a twilight world peopled by the lonely, the unwanted, and the suicidal". This may be a journalistic approach to a pressing problem, but, all the same, these are the kind of experiments which we should note with sympathetic understanding.

\* \* \* \* \*

In another part of the country I know of a mission set in the heart of a slum, whose doors are never shut by day. A constant procession of the lonely pass through to find warmth and friendship. An old woman once said to my wife, "I don't care what happens to me through the week as long as I can get to Old Folks on Thursdays." Thursday meant a warm room, much chatter among the old folk, tea drinking of course, followed by a reading from a book and a brief Epilogue. So simple was it—and yet it meant much to so many including the woman whose words I have quoted. Looking back, I am more than grateful that at that time of war and depression, we were able to do so much from that church for lonely folk of all ages and conditions.

Whilst I was in the North-east I met a man called Jack Lawson. He will not remember me, but I shall not forget him. We spoke together at a Church Anniversary. I knew him as a Methodist Local Preacher, an ex-miner and miner's leader, a Labour M.P. who had become a member of the War Cabinet. He was then the Rt. Hon. Jack Lawson. Since, he has become Lord Lawson of Beamish, and the Lord Lieutenant of Durham. All this is most remarkable, for Jack Lawson was born a Cumberland miner's son. When I knew him he still lived, when he was at home, in a little cottage in the mining village of

Beamish. Annually, on the 31st December, he conducted the Watch-night service in the tiny Methodist chapel. The folk in the village thought the world of him, and all his miner friends will tell you that Jack Lawson is unspoiled.

Many years ago he wrote something of his story in *A Man's Life*. In the book he tells of the debt that he, and others like him, owed forty and fifty years ago to those little Methodist chapels of County Durham. They were fostering places where lonely youths and maidens found themselves. The Jack Clemos of life are few: the young Jack Lawsons very many—lonely and inhibited and needing encouragement and friendship more than anything else. Here were Christian communities where youth was encouraged to exercise its gifts; to dare to sing and speak; to talk and argue, and even pray with other people. After the services a welcoming house would be invaded by a group of young people who would have supper and then spend the rest of the evening talking, or singing to their heart's content. They were, as Lawson tells you, a "merry lot" as they discussed pit-work, the Bible, ideals, books and union business, and sang and sang again. "I was given their warm, helpful friendship, and the hospitality of their homes. No longer was I 'queer' or 'alone'. My thoughts and dreams were given direction." It is true, admits Jack Lawson, that in those little Bethels there were tendencies to narrowness and hypocrisy, but these were the places, nevertheless, that opened the Infinite to the lonely and inhibited.

A group in our community much more isolated than many imagine are the deaf and dumb. I was especially delighted recently to read in a religious paper of the way a seventy-two-year-old deaf and dumb man had been made a church member. What added to my interest was that this had happened through the agency of a young man whom I had baptised twenty years before.

James Hill had been deaf and dumb for sixty of his

seventy-two years, but had kept himself wonderfully trim and cheerful in spite of the isolation brought about by his disability. Two years ago at Harvest time he sent a gift of flowers and fruit to the church close by, with a pencilled note, "For Harvest". This led to enquiries being made and, such was the spirit of this church, he was gradually drawn into its fellowship. How was this done? Two young men took the trouble to learn the deaf and dumb sign language. One of them was the young man I had christened, son of the church's minister, and the other the church's caretaker.

During the hymn singing Mr. Hill reads the words to himself, invariably finishing far in advance of the congregation, as is evidenced by the snap of his book when he reaches the end. During the sermon, he dips into the Book of Common Prayer. Then, as soon as the service is over, there is a flashing of fingers and thumbs as his two friends converse with him. They have been able to do this so well, says the report, that Mr. Hill has been able to understand the rights and duties of membership in this church, and to accept them.

\*   \*   \*   \*   \*

Some years ago I was reading a series of daily Bible studies by Dr. Alexander Findlay. When he came to the end of Chapter 18 of Matthew's Gospel he wrote "so ends the fellowship section of the Gospel, and one of the greatest chapters in the New Testament". That remark sent me back to re-read the chapter. I have studied it often since. Anyone wishing to know the mind of the Lord about the rôle of the Church should read this carefully. It reveals what should be our concern, as well as His, over the lost sheep. It tells us not to despise the weak or the insignificant. It has something to say about discipline within the fellowship, and stresses the need for, and the power of, the forgiving spirit. Would that every church would study this chapter at least once every year and absorb its teaching with each member pledging himself to live by it!

It is no accident that the *new* commandment which the Lord gave to His followers had to do with Love. He had already put His seal upon the two great Old Testament commandments, "Thou shalt love the Lord thy God with all thy heart and soul and mind and strength, and thy neighbour as thyself". Now, in the Upper Room, he adds: "A new commandment give I unto you, That ye love one another; as I have loved you, that ye also love one another." It is by this sign, He said—that of love one towards another—that men would recognize His disciples.

To observe the Lord's infinite interest in people and His compassion for them, and to realise that we are called to be His followers, is always a challenge. Can we let it be a great encouragement also? When we seek to follow Him, we do not go alone; and when we are commissioned by Him, we no longer depend merely on our own strength. The Church is meant to be a healing, reconciling fellowship, building people up; and we must do all we can to make it so. Released ourselves, it should be our joy and privilege to help to liberate others. The Church is the community with unique possibilities and a unique mission.

"Be you the new lights 'crost the valley yonder? . . . Ye aren't ever goin' to shroud 'em up—or be ye?" The point about letting our light shine, as our Lord reminds us, is that men are thus able to glorify their Father which is in heaven.

# A Final Word

*Trumpeter, sound for the splendour of God!*

.  .  .  .  .

*Trumpeter, rally us, up to the heights of it!*
*Sound for the City of God.*

ALFRED NOYES

WE have been thinking of the urgency of this problem of loneliness in the mid-20th century. Our living together in urbanised communities, the longer age-span of life under modern conditions—these make the problem increasingly acute. Unless we solve it the fact of living among greater numbers of people aggravates, instead of alleviates, our sense of isolation; and extended old age becomes a bane and not a blessing, disclosing our inner poverty.

We have noted the relation between loneliness and mental illness, neurosis, suicide and alcoholism and have realised that anything that mitigates a growing isolationism in people will help to prevent many such personal disasters. We have been impressed, too, by the suggestion that loneliness is the fundamental evil behind the major disasters of our time. Our era has witnessed wave after wave of anarchy and disorder due to the *Revolution of the Lonely*.

Looking at life in all its phases we have observed that no stage is exempt from its ravages. Loneliness attacks people of all ages and conditions; but the problem is ultimately the same—that of establishing good relationships with other people, whether they be boys and girls, or men and women. Psychology can help us from falling into many errors in this realm of inter-personal relationships. Above all religion insists that God wants us to get our relationships right with Him, with one another, and with ourselves. "Love" is life's keyword, and it is something we discover in the deepest way when sharing life with God.

The challenge to the Church is clear and obvious. Never must she become an in-growing institution. She has a mission to the world, and before her is an area of possible help to the lonely, at present only half explored. She is meant to be a means by which God's love and power can flow into a needy world. If instead of becoming a conductor she becomes an insulator, keeping people *away* from the very gifts which she exists to share, has not one of the greatest tragedies overtaken her?

For us individually there is a sure way out of loneliness. We can let love into our lives. We can find the point in our living where love's grain of mustard seed is to be found within us, and begin to foster it. We can open the doors of our inner being to the Love of God so freely offered us by Christ. Then we need be lonely no more.

*　　*　　*　　*　　*

In the last analysis, what we have been looking at is a heart-hunger which God alone can satisfy. Its various forms witness to a lack of adjustment, at some point, to His way and will, and the more we come to know of His Spirit as manifested by the Lord Jesus Christ, the more we discover the final remedy.

Indeed, the clue to our understanding of the lonely heart comes in thinking of loneliness as a "divine discontent"—part of the framework of life by which we are reminded that we are straying from life's centre. Where the Spirit of God abounds love, goodness and companionship abide.

When we find ourselves overwhelmed by a sense of separation and isolation we should take warning. Augustine's well-known saying that we human beings are restless until we find our rest in Him is profoundly true. It applies to deep loneliness especially. The nerve of our spirit is exposed, and the pain is meant to drive us into doing something about it. Our jangling restlessness will not find ultimate satisfaction anywhere else. The drugs and the quack nostrums of our own day will not deal with the problem any more than the age-long attempts to escape from it in excesses of one kind or another. They may have the effect of dulling the pain for a while, but the inner restlessness remains.

George Herbert has a poem symbolically entitled *The Pulley*. It represents God creating man, and pouring blessings on him. Before every blessing had been bestowed, however, God holds one back—the gift of rest. That He retains lest man, possessing this, should find his satisfaction in the realm of God's gifts instead of in relationship with Him, the Giver. All other blessings man may keep, says God, yet:

> *with repining restlessness.*
> *Let him be rich and weary; that, at least*
> *If goodness lead him not, yet weariness*
> *May toss him to My breast.*

There may even come a time when one or another of us at this moment deeply dissatisfied, terribly lonely, will be able to thank God for this experience. It will have brought us to a knowledge of our need of Him, and to a discovery of the well of love that is in Christ. Then, outweighing all our shyness, greater than our sense of separation, will be the new sense of involvement with our fellows. We shall see them in a new light and have in our hearts a concern for them annihilating our self-conscious isolation.

Any experience which introduces us to Him will in the

end be seen to be worth while. We need to believe that this is true even of this desperate experience of loneliness. If it can but drive us to Him, we shall find we are, in the deepest sense, "at home". Our circumstances, whatever they may be, though perhaps remaining outwardly the same, will be changed from within. Our lives, however poor we may account them, will be brought within the glow of God's abiding Presence, and something of His radiance shed abroad. Remade into the image of God, we shall be privileged to enter into His Spirit and to mirror something of His nature.

In all this, we shall come to know the power of what one in our own day has called "The Transforming Friendship". No one who has come to realise that he is companioned by the Lord at all times will any longer experience the distress of the lonely heart.

*That which we have seen and heard we proclaim also to you, so that you may have fellowship with us; and our fellowship is with the Father and with His Son Jesus Christ. And we are writing this that our joy may be complete.*